The Bond
with
the Beloved

The Bond
with
the Beloved

*The Mystical Relationship
of the Lover and the Beloved*

Llewellyn Vaughan-Lee

First published in the United States in 1993 by
The Golden Sufi Center
P.O. Box 456, Point Reyes, California 94956
www.goldensufi.org

Third Printing 2012.

Cover Image by Tennessee Dixon
Printed and Bound by Naughton & Gunn, Inc.

Library of Congress Cataloging in Publication Data

Vaughan-Lee, Llewellyn.
    The bond with the beloved : the mystical relationship of
    the lover and the beloved / Llewellyn Vaughan-Lee.
    p. cm.
    Originally published: 1993
    Includes bibliographical references and index.
    ISBN 0-9634574-0-3 (alk. paper)
    1. Mysticism. 2. Love--Religious aspects. 3. Sufism.
    4. Love--Religious aspects--Sufism. I.Title.

BL625.V38 2003
291.4'22--dc21   2003049245

ISBN 13: 978-0-9634574-0-0

Contents

Preface

Throughout this book, for reasons solely of continuity and simplicity, the masculine pronoun is used for both the seeker and the teacher. Similarly, God, the Great Beloved, is referred to as He. The Absolute Truth is neither masculine nor feminine. As much as It has a divine masculine side, so It has an awe-inspiring feminine aspect.

He loves them and they love Him.

Sura 5:54

Introduction

*Our work is the love of God. Our satisfaction
lies in submission to the Divine Embrace.*
Blessed John Ruysbroeck[1]

This book is written for the lovers of God. It is for those
who know that they are His lovers and also for those for
whom this is as yet hidden within their hearts.

There are certain souls whom God has chosen to be
His lovers. His lovers belong to Him since before the
beginning of time; to quote the Blessed John Ruysbroeck:
"Thou art Mine and I am thine: I am thine and thou art
Mine, for I have chosen thee from all Eternity."[2] The
central purpose of the lover's life is to be responsive to
the needs of love, to be receptive to the call of the
Beloved: "Our activity consists in loving God and our
fruition in enduring God and being penetrated by His
love."[3]

The lover's responsiveness to the needs of his
Beloved flows from a bond between the lover and the
Beloved that was formed before the beginning of time. Just
as a child is bonded to its mother, so is the lover bonded
to the Beloved. But the bond between the lover and the
Beloved exists on the level of the soul and it can never
be broken. This bond is imprinted in the substance of the
lover's soul.

Until now this bond has been a secret, silently shared
by those who know that they are His lovers. It is
communicated through the look of the eyes or in the

silence of a group meditation. Those who belong to Him without being consciously aware of their pre-eternal commitment respond to this bond within the heart. Their heart opens in recognition of another lover, and there is a quality of communication that only exists between those who belong to Him. There is a silent affirmation of the heart, an intimacy of the soul which has nothing to do with the personality, with age, race or sex.

The bond with the Beloved, born outside of time and space, knows no difference in culture or religion. His lovers only take on the clothing of religion or culture in order to live and work in the world undistinguished from ordinary people. In reality they belong together on an inner plane that is untouched by the divisions of this world. In the words of Rûmî, "The sect of lovers is distinct from all others; Lovers have a religion and faith all of their own."[4] In the East they were described by a term referring to their holy poverty (*darwish* in modern Persian), because the lover is someone who can only be fulfilled by the Beloved. Only by being truly poor can he be fully responsive to the needs of the Beloved. The bond with the Beloved does not belong to the world of forms, and only through inner poverty, a state of inner emptiness, can this bond fulfill its real purpose.

This book explores the meaning of this bond of love: what it means to the lover in his solitary quest for the Beloved. It is an imprinted remembrance of Him who was always with us that becomes dynamically activated when we consciously begin the spiritual quest, when we turn away from the world and begin to search for our first love. This bond holds us in the heart of the Beloved as we seek for Him. It guides us through the pain of separation and then embraces us in the bliss of union. Through it we listen to His hint and learn to follow His guidance. It is a direct link of love that becomes more and more central to the lover's life, enabling him to live in the presence of the Beloved.

But the bond with the Beloved also has a meaning beyond the individual journey of the lover. Through it the Beloved enters the lover's life and is thus able to live in His own world. This bond belongs to Him and reflects the link of love that exists between the Creator and His creation. As the lover loses himself in this link of love and experiences his natural state of holy poverty, so he becomes an empty space through which the Beloved can experience His own world and thus come to know Himself more fully, for "I was a hidden treasure, and I wanted to be known, so I created the world."

His lovers are those who in their hearts relate directly to Him. They are His servants and their work is to *consciously* recognize the link of love between the Creator and the creation; in a *hadîth* quoted by al-Ghazzâlî: "Verily I have servants among my servants who love Me, and I love them, and they long for Me, and I long for them and they look at Me, and I look at them . . . ."[5] In recognizing this link of love they hold this consciousness for the world. They belong to the Beloved and do this work for Him; they are "a brotherhood of migrants who keep watch on the world and for the world."[6]

At the present time we are in a period of global transition symbolized by the dawn of the Aquarian age. As the old structures and patterns of consciousness break down there is a need to make this bond of love conscious, to reveal this secret which has been kept hidden for so long. Humanity needs to know the strength of the link of love that binds it to the Creator. The work of His lovers is to integrate this knowledge into the collective consciousness of mankind. In order to help this to happen His lovers need to know the importance of their work.

Our Western patriarchal culture values activity above contemplation, "doing" as opposed to "being." We have thus become conditioned to think that positive participation in the present global transformation necessitates outer action in socio-ecological reform. Yet Christ, one of the greatest Western reformers, praised the tranquil Mary above the busy Martha:

> Martha, Martha, thou art careful and troubled about many things:
> But one thing is needful: and Mary hath chosen that good part, which shall not be taken away from her.[7]

Mary, sitting at the feet of Christ, had chosen the "one thing needful," contemplation above action.

The path of the lover does not reject active involvement in the world. Sufis, who were known as "lovers of God" before they were called Sufis, have always been active in the outer world. It is said that in every trouble spot in the world a Sufi is there, helping. But in all their outer work the attention of His lovers is inward, their hearts are turned towards the Beloved.

The inner attention of the lover is the "one thing needful" because it holds in the center of consciousness the "link of love which knits up reality and draws all things to their home in God."[8] At the present time of transition there is an urgent need for humanity to re-establish a conscious connection with its prime purpose as guardians of this planet. This purpose is hidden within the link of love, and manifested through the attitude of the lover. If this purpose is integrated within the collective consciousness of humanity then the coming age will see humanity awakening out of the egotistic greed that has almost destroyed the planet.

Outer circumstances point to the need for global responsibility, but this responsibility needs to be founded on a purpose beyond survival. Mankind's ego drives are so strong and divisive that a unified global consciousness will only function if it is based upon the divine consciousness of the Self, which is a natural state of unified consciousness that is the very foundation of our psychic structure. The Self is the part of mankind that is not separate from the Creator. It is both a higher center of consciousness within the individual and also a collective consciousness in which all of life is part of an integrated whole. At the level of the Self the consciousness of the individual is united with the greater consciousness of the whole. Then the individual realizes the unity of life not as a concept but as a dynamic reality.

During each period of transition, whether on a personal or collective level, as the old structures break down and before new structures are formed, a space opens up for a higher level of consciousness to be integrated. The higher consciousness of the Self is the hidden agent of transformation, always helping humanity to grow into a new awareness. But after the time of transition it is usually buried again beneath new structures of ego conditioning, in the same way that a religion loses its initial integrity when it becomes a socio-political organization. At the present time a higher consciousness is surfacing, manifesting as an awareness of the need for a global approach to present problems.

The work of His lovers is to integrate the higher consciousness of the Self into the collective consciousness of mankind before this collective consciousness is again crystallized into patterns of ego-gratification. The Self embraces all aspects of life and at the same time carries the hidden purpose of creation and our role as guardians of the planet. His lovers can help humanity remember its hidden purpose which is held in trust by the Self.

For centuries His lovers have worked alone or in small groups, bringing His light into their immediate environment. Often His lovers did not even know themselves what work they were doing—the work of the heart is often kept hidden from the interference of the mind and the ego. The lover is but a pen in the hands of the Beloved. But at the present time His lovers need to know that they are working towards a collective purpose. The lover's inner attention on the Beloved forms a point of light in the world that now forms part of a web of light that is being woven around the world.

It is this web of light that has the potential to hold the higher consciousness of the Self within the collective consciousness of the world. This web of light can be the foundation of a new level of collective consciousness which continually remembers the oneness of life. An opportunity is arising for the world to open to God and recognize that it embodies His oneness. Then the world as a whole could be imprinted with a conscious aware-ness of its link with the Beloved. It is the communion of lovers that holds open the heart of the world, so that if it is His will He can engrave His own creation with His name in the same way that He has engraved His name upon the hearts of His lovers.

THE SHADOW SIDE
OF
SPIRITUAL LIFE

The thing we tell of can never be found by seeking,
yet only seekers find it.
Abû Yazîd 'l-Bistâmî

THERE IS NO GOD BUT GOD.

Sufis believe in the Oneness of Being because there is
nothing other than God. This quintessential truth is
expressed in the *shahâdu*, the saying "*Lâ ilâha illâ 'llâh*"
("There is no god but God"). In the depths of our heart
we know this, for this is the secret covenant between the
Creator and His creation. We know that we are not other
than God. The aim of every mystical path is to return to
this primal knowledge, to know what we knew before
we experienced separation from God.[1]

This truth is hidden like an embryo within us. It is
the essence of consciousness. In our normal understanding, consciousness necessitates duality, the separation of
subject and object. If there is no differentiation there is no
consciousness. We know and identify things by their
differences. Everything that has been created is distinct
and individual; no two leaves are the same. But the
mystic knows that consciousness has another dimension
in which things are known not because they are separate,

but because they are all one: "In our hall of mirrors, the map of one Face appears."² The recognition of oneness within multiplicity is the recognition of the Creator manifest in the creation. It is the real purpose of consciousness, as expressed in the Qur'an, Sura 7:172, when "before creation, God called the future humanity out of the loins of the not yet created Adam, and addressed them with the words: 'Am I not your Lord ?' (*alastu bi-rabbikum*) and they answered: 'Yes, we witness it' (*balâ shahidnâ*)."³ The witness (*shâhid*) is the one who sees God in everything.

Paradoxically, in order to realize this state of consciousness we have to lose it. We have to experience separation from God in order to realize that we are never separate from God. The mystic is one who comes into this world with the prime purpose of rediscovering this state of union and then living it. In being born he surrenders himself to the pain of separation in order that he may come to know God more fully, may come to know God as He has revealed Himself in His creation. In His creation God has manifested both His eternal Majesty (*jalâl*) and His eternal Beauty (*jamâl*), and so allowed Himself to be known more completely. At the core of creation He has hidden an innermost secret aspect of Himself. The mystic's purpose is to discover this secret and offer it back to the Beloved. This secret cannot be told in words, but it is contained in the whole mystery of the mystic's return journey.

The journey from God back to God embraces the painful process of separation. Leaving the state of uncreated oneness we come into this world and are engulfed in forgetfulness. In being born we give ourself into this unknowing, this separation from the direct knowledge of God. But at the same time we carry within us the deep bond of the lover and the Beloved; "In memory of the Beloved we quaffed a vintage that made us drunk before the creation of the vine."[4] This bond manifests as the sigh of the soul, the longing which is not only the pain of separation but also the knowledge of Him from whom we are separated. Without this knowledge there would be no pain. At the core of the longing is the knowledge that there is no separation, that the lover and the Beloved are always united. It is this paradox that burns within the heart of the seeker: we are united and yet we are separate, there is only oneness and yet we are caught in duality. This is the same as the paradox that consciousness necessitates separation and yet the highest form of consciousness is that there is no separation.

Those who make the painful journey home do so because they have not entirely forgotten this home. When they came into this world they kept part of the consciousness of union. This is both a blessing and a curse. It is a blessing because it does not allow us to become entirely engulfed in the things of this world, lost in the temptations of Maya. However involved we become in our outer surroundings there is always the feeling that this is not everything, that something more important is waiting for us. But this is a curse because it makes us feel that we do not fit in, we are always a stranger in this world. Often we do not know the reason for this, we do not know that it is because we are inwardly so close to the Beloved that He does not let us forget Him. We think that it is a fault or failure that we want something other than what the world has to offer. It can be particularly painful when we have parents who cannot understand this deeper need, and may even be jealous of what they sense to be an inner connection to something beyond their grasp.

One friend waited till she was over forty before she reconnected with an inner closeness that she had as a

child. Then she dreamt a long and complicated psychological dream at the end of which she saw a figure
standing in a doorway. Working with the dream she
recognized that this figure was her "first love." First she
associated her father as this first love, but then realized
that it was not he but her relationship to God. As a child
she had a very direct relationship with the Beloved. But
her father, wanting her love for himself, sensed this
deeper love, grew jealous of it and thus caused her to
repress it. For many painful empty years she lived
isolated from the one relationship that had real meaning.
But then her first love returned, standing in a doorway,
silently calling her back inside herself. He had always
been waiting there, waiting for her to turn back to the
bliss and the pain that is love's promise:

> The minute I heard my first love story
> I started looking for you, not knowing
> how blind that was.
> Lovers don't finally meet somewhere.
> They're in each other all along.[5]

For another friend it was her mother who caused her
to deny her spirituality; threatened by her daughter's
knowledge of an inner softness that was unobtainable to
her, she continually attacked her daughter's inner relationship. Driven by despair into depression, the daughter
tried to give up her spirituality in order to live a normal,
socially acceptable life. For a few years this seemed to
work, but underneath life became meaningless. Life
became so empty that there came the point where she
would have died if she had not given herself to her inner
vision. For those who carry the curse of remembrance
spiritual life is not a choice but a deep and painful need,
an open wound that can only be healed by the Beloved.

The memory of the beyond is like the grain of sand in the oyster shell that creates the pearl. It causes a painful friction between the outer world and the inner world. The stronger the memory, the greater the friction. Then one day this friction creates a fire that we cannot ignore. It is then that the spiritual quest begins in earnest. It is then that we consciously turn away from the outer world and seek the invisible source of our pain.

TURNING AWAY FROM THE WORLD

Traditionally the first stage on the Sufi path is *tauba*. Translated literally *tauba* means "repentance or change of heart." Yet this is misleading because in the religious context repentance means: "If I did something wrong I promise I'll repent, do some penance and promise not to do it again." But in the mystical context *tauba* is a turning of the heart. It is a spiritual awakening that can be triggered by an outer event or an inner happening, a dream or vision. When I was sixteen I happened to read a Zen saying,

> The wild geese do not intend to cast their reflection,
> The water has no mind to receive their image.

This saying was like a key that opened an inner door, and for two weeks I laughed with the joy of the soul at what I saw. I started to meditate and discovered a reality that was more powerful and more meaningful than an outer world in which I came to realize I had long felt a stranger. Many years later I discovered that this was also a favorite saying of Bhai Sahib, the Sufi Master in *Daughter of Fire*. He would also often liken the enigmatic nature of the path to that of birds in flight, "Look at the birds in the sky.

5

Can you trace the path of their flight?"

The initial awakening of the seeker is a momentary glimpse of a different reality. It is always a gift and cannot be brought about by the desire of the student. Someone once asked Râbi'a:

> "I have committed many sins; if I turn in penitence towards God, will He turn in mercy towards me?"
>
> "No," she replied, "but if He shall turn towards you, you will turn towards Him."[6]

The spiritual quest is a response to a call: because He calls us to Him we turn away from the world to seek Him. Then begins the long and lonely journey home, the "flight of the alone to the Alone."

His call catalyses a spiritual instinct that is within us. Every human being comes into this world with two primary instincts: the will to live and the will to worship. It is this latter instinct that is so dynamically awakened by the Beloved that we are no longer content to worship Him, but we need to unite with Him. The seventeenth-century contemplative, Jeanne Guyon, describes this instinctual awakening:

> As soon as God touches a seeker, He gives that new believer an instinct to return to Him more perfectly and be united with Him. There is something within the believer that knows he has not been created for amusement or the trivals of the world but has an end which is centered in His Lord. Something within the believer endeavours to cause him to return to a place deep within, to a place of rest. It is an instinctive thing, this pull to return to God. Some receive it in a larger portion, accord-

ing to God's design, others to a smaller degree, by God's design. But each believer has that loving impatience to return to his source of origin.[7]

The Beloved has awakened his lover to the deepest need of the soul, to the hunger that is the driving force of the seeker: "Nourish me for I am hungry and hurry for time is a sword."[8] This hunger is the instinctual core of the spiritual journey and is often accompanied by a despair that it will never be satisfied. Spiritual life is a craving that cannot be satisfied by anything which the world has to offer, and its awakening can often be terrifying to the ego. For some people the experience of *tauba* simply makes sense of a meaningless life and they are only too glad to turn away from a world from which they already felt alienated. But there are also those who have struggled long and hard to realize their own independence and have made a successful life in worldly terms. Hearing His call resonate within their own hearts they know what it means. They know that everything for which they have struggled will be taken away, not just attachments to the material world, but also the sense of being able to determine one's own life. It is this latter illusion of freedom or self-determination, which in the West we value so highly, that is often the most difficult to surrender. Although the only real freedom comes from the surrender of the ego to the Self, the ego resists this with all its strength and powers of persuasion. Thus the seeker is torn between his response to the Beloved's call and his awareness of what this means. Yet the very fact that spiritual life evokes such a conflict and often a lengthy struggle of avoidance arises precisely from the individual's deep commitment, and his knowledge that once he walks through this door he will enter the arena of his own death.

Turning away from the world is embodied in the first part of the *shahâda, Lâ ilâha*, "there is no God." This is the principle of negation, for every spiritual path teaches that the goal is not to be found in the outer world, but within: "the kingdom of God is within you." Thus when we step upon the path our attention is turned from the outer world to the inner world. From the depths of our heart He calls us and through the spiritual techniques of the path we learn how to come towards Him, how to enter the inner world. Meditation is usually the most important practice, for it refocuses the seeker, first by stilling the outward activity of the mind and then awakening him to inner experiences. Other spiritual practices can have a similar effect. In particular the *dhikr*, the repetition of the name of God, keeps the inner attention of the wayfarer away from the world and turned towards God.

Being part of a spiritual group and sitting in the presence of a teacher can also help to keep the wayfarer focused on the inner direction of his quest. The teacher and the group, charged with the energy of the path, function as a magnet, attracting the inner attention of the seeker and pointing it towards the heart. On a more conscious level the presence of others for whom the inner quest is a real and serious undertaking helps to reinforce the individual's sense of purpose. Sitting with a group in meditation is a powerful reminder of a shared vision which beckons from the inner world. Similarly, the tradition and spiritual lineage of the teacher and the group support the wayfarer with the invisible presence of all those who have travelled this path in preceding centuries. The world's spiritual literature, which is now available as never before, also helps the individual to realize that his own desire for the beyond is a part of mankind's collective spiritual journey, which has always affirmed that Truth is an inner reality far transcending anything that can be found in the outer world.

All this support is particularly important in our Western materialistic culture which collectively denies the value if not the very existence of the inner world. It gives the wayfarer an identity and a sense of belonging which is needed in the most difficult first stages of the path. The initial experience of *tauba* turns our attention away from the world. We then consciously take up the role of the seeker, the spiritual wayfarer making the journey back to the Beloved. This journey appears to begin with His call that awakens us, and yet He only calls those who already belong to Him, whom He has sent out into the world in order to reveal the secret hidden in creation. Once I attended a conference in which some-one asked, "How do you become a Sufi?" A member of the audience who consciously knew nothing about Sufism instinctively answered, "As far as I understand you do not become a Sufi. You always were a Sufi but didn't know it." Three years later the woman who gave this correct reply had a dream in which she was invited to join a circle of white-clad figures. When she told the dream she suddenly realized what she had long suspected, that she had always been a Sufi. But this dream signalled that now was the time for her to fully recognize this.

The journey home began the moment we left the state in which we knew we were not other than He. We surrendered ourselves into forgetfulness in order that He can know Himself more fully when we open our eyes and return to Him. Yet although this return journey begins with the moment of separation, for many years it is unconscious, hidden beneath the illusion of the world. The experience of *tauba* is the shock that brings this journey into consciousness. When the Beloved calls to us, the bond that exists and has always existed, outside of time and space, between the lover and the Beloved, is charged with the energy of love, allowing the higher consciousness of the Self to break through into ordinary consciousness. This creates a momentary awareness of our union with the Beloved that awakens us to the pain of our separation and forgetfulness.

In the moment of awakening the Beloved is present with us as never before. In this moment we consciously know that we are both separate and united with Him. As human beings we carry the consciousness of God, for our consciousness is part of the divine consciousness. It is His greatest gift which distinguishes us from the other forms of life on this planet. Thus, in this moment of awakening He makes known His purpose to Himself. He reveals to Himself the hidden mystery of creation which contains His experience of the pain of separation. Our longing to be reunited with God is none other than His own longing:

> It is he who suffers his absence in me
> Who through me cries out to himself.
> Love's most strange, most holy mystery—
> We are intimate beyond belief.[9]

The lover has this most intimate relationship with the Beloved. In our longing we experience that He too is lonely, for He desires us more than we can ever know. In our desire to go home He shares this secret with us: that although He is perfect He needs us. He needs us because we are imperfect and can share this mystery with Him.

In the world that reflects His oneness all things are different. No two moments are the same and each petal of the rose has a different shape and a different color. In this world created by Him who is perfect nothing is perfect, as the oriental-carpet makers acknowledge when they purposefully include an imperfection in their design. This is the paradox of creation: He who is One comes to know Himself through multiplicity. He who is perfect sees Himself in the mirror of imperfection.

Our awareness of our own imperfection depends upon our deeper awareness of His perfection. It is because we remember the state of perfection when we were not separate from Him, that our imperfection carries the hidden anguish of separation. Our own imperfection is most painfully evident in the experience of love. This energy, which al-Hallâj describes as "the essence of the essence of God and the mystery of creation,"[10] continually confronts us with our faults; it is said in the *Kama Sutra* that "love without conflict is not of this world." Creation contains the opposites and the conflict between them in which the web of imperfection is woven. Without imperfection there would be no evolution; for the seeker it is the awareness of his own faults that makes him experience the primal conflict of light and dark, good and bad.

Energy is born from opposites, from the dynamic interplay of positive and negative. This is why the awakening is characterized as "repentance," for it is an awareness of our faults in contrast to the perfection of our Beloved that generates the energy that transforms us. Thrown between the opposites, burnt by the awareness of our own darkness and our longing for His light, we experience the birth pain of consciousness: that He created darkness in us in order that we might come to know Him better. He embraces the opposites while we are caught in their conflict. To quote Rûmî, "Everything is good and perfect in relation to God but not in relation to us."[11]

Facing our darkness we struggle towards the light. Finally, worn away by the conflict the ego surrenders and

11

we are taken beyond these opposites. Just as we first awoke to the pain of separation and the darkness of the lover's imperfection, so do we awaken to the higher consciousness of the Self that experiences the oneness in everything. People often have dreams of the teacher acting in an improper way, swearing in a church, smoking in a meditation room, in order to shock them into an awareness of this higher reality. The perfect man embraces both his own imperfection and also that of mankind. This is illustrated in the story of Jâmî who was mistaken for a thief. On being asked if he was a thief the saint replied, "What am I not?"

TURNING BACK TO GOD

The path that begins and ends in oneness confronts the wayfarer with the duality of the world and God. Seeking the Beloved we have turned away from the world and now turn back to God. This is the second part of the *shahâda, illâ 'llâh* (but God), the affirmation. It evokes an intense struggle as the ego and the mind hold onto the known values and structures of the outer world, resisting the pull of the heart and its deep desire for the formless inner world.

But the affirmation is also a conscious identification with the quest and our desire for the Beloved. To help us in the struggle of turning back to God we give ourselves an identity as a wayfarer, a spiritual seeker. Rather than just confronting the total nothingness of spiritual truth in which the ego is annihilated, we give our conscious self something to hold onto, a ladder of ascent that can take us from the world of forms into the formless. This idea of a spiritual identity is essentially a trick to help the ego to loosen its hold on the world. The goal is to become "featureless and formless," to lose every name until only His name remains. For this reason when Irina Tweedie asked her Sufi Master, Bhai Sahib, about being initiated as a disciple, he replied, "It is not for you." And she realized "it would be in contradiction with what I am trying to do, namely grappling with the gigantic task of learning how to become nothing."[12] But this process of annihilation takes time. It is a gradual death. It is said in the Upanishads that if you want Truth as badly as a drowning man wants air you will realize it in a split second. But who wants Truth as much as that? Before we surrender to the bottomless void that is beyond the mind we have to make the slow ascent that is our own crucifixion.

When the Buddhist scriptures were first taken from India to China it was discovered before they were delivered that the scrolls were blank. These blank scrolls contained the real spiritual Truth, but just as only Ananda understood when Buddha silently held up a flower, humanity needs to approach the great void more gradually. Scrolls with writing were substituted to help the seeker define the inner path.

When we first turn back to the Beloved we think of ourself as a wayfarer traveling a path. Gradually we realize that this pathless path is none other than our own inner being calling out to ourself. Then the wayfarer and the path cease to be a duality. Finally they both disappear. But the idea of being a wayfarer on a path is a necessary illusion to help us cross over to a world beyond the ego.

An essential part of this "crossing" is the focus on the Beloved. We cannot turn away from the world unless we turn towards God. We can only free ourselves from the desires that imprison us in this world through the greater desire that we have for God. We escape from the gravitational pull of the earth by consciously aligning ourselves with the greater gravitational pull of the sun of suns. The affirmation, *illâ 'llâh*, is a one-hundred-eighty-degree turn in which we realign ourselves with the energy of the Self that transforms us. Part of this realigning is the conscious recognition that Truth is an inner reality. The one-hundred-eighty-degree turn is thus a turn from the outer world to the inner world. It is a conscious commitment to an inner journey. In the words of Saint Augustine, "Return within yourself. In the inward man dwells truth."[13]

ISOLATION AND THE SHAME OF SPIRITUALITY

At the beginning there is a painful period of detachment as old values fall away. We often need more time to be alone and may need to change our style of living. Slowly the outer world loses its attraction and this may also happen with old friends and old habits. Our focus has been redirected, and people and activities that used to interest us no longer hold our attention. Similarly we can appear boring to people who are only interested in outer stimuli. Those whose identity and self-worth are determined solely by the outer world may even be threatened by the silent voice of one who looks elsewhere, who seeks to lose the ego rather than to gratify it. This is why a spiritual group is so valuable, providing a sense of community in a world from which the seeker can feel increasingly isolated.

This sense of isolation is emphasized by our Western culture because it has long denied the mystic. Since its early struggles against the gnostics, the Christian church has rejected the individual quest in favor of social and political power. Where is the wandering dervish or orange-robed sanyasin of our culture? The seeker's tendency towards isolation is even more emphasized in the United States, which, being the most extrovert society in the world, has little sympathy for the introvert path of the mystic.

Only too often the outcast carries the shadow of the culture, which in this case is the unrecognized longing for something beyond the material world. Those who belong to the Beloved carry His curse which is the memory of His embrace. Nothing in the world will fulfill them. But when this curse is combined with the collective shadow it can easily become a feeling of shame. How many children are silently worried because they see a world invisible to their parents? How many adolescents bury their spirituality because it has no echo? These feelings fester in the darkness. They become the secret shame of the shadow. We sense the emptiness of material values. We see that the emperor has no clothes. But without an outer context to contain or help us understand this insight we are left only with the primal guilt of consciousness. Spirituality thus carries a double curse.

A friend who was confronted with accepting her spirituality had a dream in which she let a cat out of a bag. She revealed her secret which had been contained in guilt. At the same time an unconscious feeling that she would be punished surfaced, for the collective shadow carries the danger of persecution; and our collective history is only too full of persecuting true spirituality. During the period of owning one's inner aspirations the support of a spiritual group is invaluable, for then the shameful feelings are shared and taken away. The seeker is accepted within a circle of friends, within a peer group of souls.

Wayfarers are always attracted to those with whom they have an inner empathy. This is the hidden resonance of a Sufi group which is recognized by those who belong. It is a collective memory of the Beloved, a shared silent longing. Abû Sa'îd ibn Abî'l-Khayr describes the origin of these groups of friends:

> Four thousand years before God created these bodies, he created the souls and kept them beside himself and shed a light upon them. He knew what quantity each soul received and he showed favor to each in proportion to its illumination. The souls remained all that time in light, until they became fully nourished. Those who in this world live in joy and agreement with one another must have been akin to one another in that place. Here they love one another and are called the friends of God, and they are brothers who love one another for God's sake. These souls know one another by smell, like horses.[14]

When we find such friends we are like the ugly duckling who saw the swans and then recognized his own reflection. The sense of relief can be tremendous. We have found a support that we need to help us on the inner journey. We can confront our own wounds without being overwhelmed by them. We see God's curse for the blessing it is. We recognize our longing as the song that will take us home.

THE JOURNEY IN GOD

Our face is now turned towards the Beloved and He calls us to Him. He begins to share with His lover the mysteries of love. In the tenderest, innermost places of our heart He touches us. He opens us to Him, slowly lifting the veils that separate us. In these moments of intimacy the world disappears. Human lovers experience the passion and tenderness of union in privacy. Closing out the clamour of the world two people give themselves to an ecstasy that takes them into the beyond. But human passion is just an echo of the passion of the soul for the Beloved. It is here, on the inner stage, that the real ecstasy is experienced, as lover and Beloved merge without the separation of bodies.

We learn to long for the night, when the distractions of the world disappear and there is time for silence and the communion of lovers:

> O God, the stars are shining:
> All eyes have closed in sleep;
> The kings have locked their doors.
> Each lover is alone, in secret, with the one he loves.
> And I am here too: alone, hidden from all of them—
> With You.[15]

Each moment that we can withdraw from the world is precious, for there is the possibility of meeting. We look for Him everywhere, but in the world He is so hidden. In the moments of meditation He comes closer. This is the secret of the lover, that when we look within He may be waiting. What do we want of the world when we know His touch, the gentlest of butterfly wings on the edge of our heart? Even the memory of such tenderness can incite passion. In a moment He can fill us to overflowing and make us forget that we ever left His arms.

But these meetings make the world a cold and empty place. We wait for nightfall, hoping that He will be there again. In the intervening hours we live as best we can, remembering Him. Driving on the freeway, working in the office, we perform our worldly duties but they seem without purpose. We feel we are caught between the two worlds, often unable to reconcile their opposition: the endless expanses of the heart with the restrictions of time and space. We live and work in a world that carries preoccupations about money, but what does the soul care about such things?

THE CONSTELLATION OF THE SHADOW

The journey towards oneness emphasizes the opposites and we are caught in their conflict. We live in this world and have work and responsibilities, families and mortgages that demand our attention. Yet we long for something else. This tension between the opposites creates a painful but transformative dynamic. It involves living the primal contradiction of incarnation: that we are both divine and human. As the inner experiences intensify so this contradiction can be more painful. We glimpse the dimension of the soul and are then thrown back into the world. This only increases our longing, the feeling of separation that burns us and pulls us to the Beloved.

The deeper the experiences with the Beloved the more painful the separation. The world seems the cause of this separation. It distracts us from our inner quest. In the early centuries of Islam some Sufis sought to avoid any such distraction by taking the path of the ascetic. With a brick for a pillow and a worn-out straw mat for a bed, they despised this world, which they considered a dangerous snare on the way to God. Even work was a distraction from their inner attention. The path of the ascetic does not belong to the present time (see pp. 24-

25) and in fact many Sufis have stressed the importance of inner detachment, the poverty of the heart rather than outer poverty. However, the ascetic's attitude can be seen today reflected in the way seekers easily despise the mundane activities of life, and would like to escape from the time-consuming concerns that are a part of living in our present world.

Yet there is a psychological law that states that every stance of consciousness constellates its opposite in the unconscious. The moment we turn away from the world and look towards God our shadow falls behind us. Our view of the world then becomes contaminated by our own shadow. What we despise is our own ordinary self. When we turned towards the Beloved we left part of ourself behind, the part that we did not associate with the quest. At the beginning this is necessary. It is an effect of the process of negation and affirmation. We negate the aspect of ourself which we identify as worldly in order to affirm our spiritual nature. As I have mentioned this new spiritual identification is a crutch to help free us from the attraction of the world and focus our attention on the Beloved. But the price that we pay for this crutch is the projection of our shadow onto the world.

In fact our ordinary, worldly self can be helpful on the path. In the ninth century the Sufis of Nîshâpûr realized the danger inherent in becoming identified as a wayfarer, for this very identity strengthens the ego. Many Sufis of that time could be recognized by the special patch-frock garments that they wore, and so the Nîshâpûr Sufis only wore ordinary clothes. This attitude became integrated into the Naqshbandi tradition, which stressed the idea of "solitude in the crowd"—"outwardly to be with the people, inwardly to be with God." Naqshbandi Sufis do not dress differently from others and externally live ordinary lives within the community. Irina Tweedie told me that the greengrocer who lived at the end of Bhai Sahib's street did not even know that Bhai Sahib was a Sufi teacher.

The less visible and the more introverted the spiritual path, the less easy it is for the ego to become over-identified and thus interfere with this journey. Thus, while other Sufi orders often chant the *dhikr,* or practice their meditation with music or dance, the Naqshbandiyya has no outward rituals. They practice the silent *dhikr* and the silent meditation of the heart.

The Sufis of Nîshâpûr also realized that the less the wayfarer knows about his own spiritual progress the better. A friend had a dream in which she was with a group of people and a teacher figure was going 'round telling each person how he or she was getting on. But when the teacher came to her she was made deaf and never heard a word. Only when the teacher passed on to the next person could she hear again. In the journey towards annihilation and nothingness it is best not to know where we are. Irina Tweedie always said, "We are just disciples of God; sinners trying to do better."

However, we cannot escape the fact that as we progress along the path and have spiritual experiences the ego can identify itself with these experiences. Although our meetings with the Beloved belong to the level of the soul, as we taste their sweetness it is only too easy for the ego to think, "I had a spiritual experience." Then the ego becomes inflated. Thinking you are progressing creates moments of elation, of greatness, fleeting feelings of divinity. Then you become unbalanced. At these moments the conflicts and difficulties of our ordinary everyday life are invaluable. How can you be a spiritually advanced person when you get angry about a parking ticket? The world continually confronts us with our failings and inadequacies and thus protects us from the dangers of inflation. It presents us with our worldly shadow that we need for balance.

Through the shadow we learn the wisdom of humility. This allows us to live in the presence of God. A disciple asked a learned rabbi why it is that God used to speak directly to his people, yet he never does so today. The wise man replied, "Man cannot bend low enough to hear what God says."[16] Humility helps us to keep out of the way, for it is only the ego that separates us from the Beloved—in the words of Abû Yazîd, "The way to God is but one step, taking one step out of oneself."

EMBRACING THE SHADOW

The shadow also carries the transformative potential of our own wholeness. As we embrace our worldly shadow we embrace the paradox that we are both human and divine. This is expressed in the Sufi saying, "He who has realized his humanness has realized his divinity." But what is important to realize is that accepting the shadow does not mean becoming identified with it. Jung once said that you do not have a shadow but the shadow has you. Most people are possessed by their shadow. In our journey along the path we have been touched by the greater wholeness of the Self which allows us to accept the shadow without losing ourself in its darkness. In accepting our worldly self we do not have to lose our spirituality and become caught in the world's desires and illusions.

In turning away from the world we gradually break the patterns of ego-identity with worldly values and instead identify with the Beloved. The Self calls to us and we respond, turning our attention inward. This creates a conscious link with the Self and the energy of the path.

Our desire for Truth, which had been hidden in the depths of the unconscious, slowly manifests its energy in our daily life, making it more difficult to keep our attention focused on our everyday duties. This energy, this deepest desire of the soul, dissolves the bonds that tie us to this world, allowing us to journey into the beyond.

As the old patterns of ego-identity break up so the deeper identity of the Self begins to surface. We do not identify with the Self—the ego cannot grasp this greater dimension. But the ego is contained within it and is slowly transformed. Eventually the ego does not battle the Self but surrenders itself into being a vehicle for the Beloved to experience His world: "My servant ceases not to draw nigh unto Me by works of devotion, until I love him, and when I love him I am the eye by which he sees and the ear by which he hears."[17] This *hadîth qudsî* (extra-Qur'anic revelation) outlines the process through which the conscious aspirations of the wayfarer, "the works of devotion," attune him to the bond of love that has existed between the Beloved and His lover *since before the beginning of time.* The recognition of this bond of love is the most powerful transformative agent on the path. It gives the wayfarer the inner security to surrender the ego and become absorbed in the Beloved.

This bond of love is the essence of the path. It is expressed in the Qur'an by the simple statement, "He loves them and they love Him" (Sura 5:59). Although this bond is between the Beloved and the lover it is reflected in the relationship between the teacher and the wayfarer, which is a bond of love that exists on the level of the soul and is therefore also outside of time. The relationship with the teacher allows us to recognize our bond with the Beloved and integrate it into our everyday life. The physical presence of the teacher bridges the gap between our eternal and temporal self, making it easier for our higher Self to manifest. As I have discussed in detail in *The Call and the Echo,*[18] this relationship also allows the wayfarer to project the higher Self onto the teacher and then reclaim this projection.

The wayfarer is contained within the heart of the teacher who is contained within the heart of the Beloved. The bond of lover and Beloved is an embrace that contains everything within it. At the beginning the wayfarer supposes that only the spiritual aspects of himself are accepted. Later we come to realize that the Beloved loves us in our entirety. This is when we glimpse life from the dimension of the Self.

Grounded on the rock of the Self the wayfarer begins to be turned back to the world to reclaim what had been rejected. The journey towards wholeness demands that this shadow be integrated. In the alchemical *opus* there is the process of *separatio* as the opposites are constellated and made conscious. But this is followed by the *coniunctio*, the union of these same opposites. The world is not other than the Beloved, and the bond between the Beloved and His lover is also the bond between the Creator and His creation. It is the wayfarer's recognition of his bond with the Beloved that enables him to see this secret hidden in creation. In our own ordinary everyday self we feel the pain of the Beloved's separation from Himself. Through our experience of this separation we glimpse the deeper mystery of His unity, that "everything is He" as Jâmî exclaims:

> Neighbour and associate and companion—everything is He.
> In the beggar's coarse frock and the king's silk—everything is He.

> In the crowd of separation and in the lone-
> liness of collectedness
> By God! everything is He, and by God! every-
> thing is He.[19]

THE INTEGRATION OF THE SHADOW
AND THE BIRTH OF JOY

The last two thousand years, the Piscean era, have been dominated by the process of *separatio*. The sign of Pisces is two fish, a duality which in the West we have experienced as the separation of spirit and matter, mind and body, conscious and unconscious. The separation into opposites evokes the constellation of the shadow; thus the physical world, which since time immemorial has been identified with the feminine, has carried both the darkness of the rejected feminine and the shadow side of the spiritual quest.

The collective drive towards *separatio*, together with this double shadow projection, has emphasized the outer dynamic of turning away from the world in the spiritual life of the last age. This can be seen in the Christian and Islamic ascetic movements of the first millennium, whose despising of the world clearly points beyond a simple negation to the activation of the shadow. Later the same shadow is evident in the way the Christian Church became possessed by the desire for wealth and power. In both instances, whether in the drive to reject the world or in being possessed by it, it is this shadow that has claimed our attention.

If the age of Pisces was concerned with the separation into opposites, then the coming age looks towards their reconciliation:

> If, as seems probable, the aeon of the fishes is
> ruled by the archetypal motif of the hostile broth-
> ers, then the approach of the next platonic month,
> namely Aquarius, will constellate the problem of
> the union of opposites.[20]

The first step towards the union of opposites is the
integration of the shadow. We can no longer afford to let
the outer world carry our shadow. Not only has our greed
almost destroyed the planet, but in our Western culture
life needs an infusion of spirit in order to make it
meaningful again.

The integration of the shadow is an act of love that
unites the opposites on a higher plane. It activates the
Self, which is symbolized by the *coniunctio*. The drive
that is surfacing within our collective psyche is the
integration of the opposites and the birth of the Self. The
work of His lovers is to infuse love into this union, so that
the child of the future vibrates with the higher frequency
of the Self.

In previous centuries the external focus of the
wayfarer on turning away from the world often lasted for
many years. Abu Sa'îd ibn Abî'l Khayr spent decades in
the desert before he returned to the world and founded
one of the first Sufi places for retreat and seclusion
(*khâneqâh*). But, as I was once told in a dream, "the
desert is no longer a spiritual place." Today the whole
inner process of negation and affirmation needs to take
place within the marketplace. From the moment of
tauba, when the heart is turned towards the Beloved, the
Sufi's work is to reflect His love into the world. This
means containing within the heart the opposites of the
inner and outer world, so that the shadow is no longer
projected but transformed. Inwardly the wayfarer will
look towards the Beloved, outwardly he will look to-

wards the world. As the wayfarer polishes the mirror of the heart, cleansing the psyche of the attachments of the ego, so the outer world will begin to reflect the face of the Beloved, for, in the words of the Qur'an, "Wheresoever you turn, there is His Face" (Sura 2:115).

As we silently work upon ourselves, the energy of our devotion becomes a point of light within the world. At the present time a map is being unfolded made of the lights of the lovers of God. The purpose of this map is to change the inner energy structure of the planet. In previous ages this energy structure was held by sacred places, stone circles, temples and cathedrals. In the next stage of our collective evolution it is the hearts of individuals that will hold the cosmic note of the planet. This note can be recognized as a song being born within the hearts of seekers. It is a quality of joy that is being infused into the world. It is the heartbeat of the world and needs to be heard in our cities and towns.

The primordial covenant in which humanity, in response to God's "Am I not your Lord?" replied "Yes, we witness it," is not just a conscious recognition of the divine, but a song of celebration, "Glory be to God," that sings in the blood as well as in the innermost recesses of the heart. This song is the manifestation of the bond between the lover and the Beloved. It is the affirmation of love, the primordial "Yes" which His lovers remember and witness. Until now this "Yes" has been a hidden secret shared silently in the hearts of those who know Him. But the time has now come for it to be heard in the marketplace as a passionate participation in life. This is what Molly Bloom exclaims at the end of James Joyce's *Ulysses*:

> O and the sea the sea crimson sometimes like
> fire and the glorious sunsets and the fig trees in the
> Alameda gardens yes and all the queer little streets

and pink and blue and yellow houses and rose
gardens and the jessamine and geranium and
cactuses and Gibraltar as a girl where I was flower
of the mountains yes when I put the rose in my
hair like the Andalusian girls used or shall I wear
a red yes and how he kissed me under the Moorish
wall and I thought well as well him as another and
then I asked him with my eyes to ask again yes and
then he asked me would I yes to say yes my
mountain flower and first I put my arms around
him yes and drew him down to me so he could
feel my breasts all perfume yes and his heart was
going like mad and yes I said yes I will Yes.

The whole world is His lover and it longs to be reunited
with Him. Every atom unknowingly sings the song of
separation and the affirmation of union. But in the hearts
of His lovers this paradox is a burning passion. They have
tasted the wine of separation and the cry of their hearts
affirms this. They know the pain of separation and they
know that He is One. It is this knowledge that is needed
to attune the whole planet.

The world has experienced *separatio* and is now
turning towards union. It is turning back towards God
and needs to know its direction. It is for this reason that
His lovers who for so long have mainly kept themselves
hidden, so that their work would not be interfered with,
now need to come into the open. Although they may be
unnoticed, their hearts will be heard; their "Yes" will
resonate and open others to the mystery of belonging. It
is this sense of belonging that allows the joy of the soul
to flow into the world. This joy is the affirmation of life
as it turns towards God. At its deepest level it is the joy
of the world becoming conscious of its true purpose as
a mirror in which the Beloved can see His own face.

PREGNANT WITH GOD

It takes time to make a soul pregnant with God.
Bhai Sahib[1]

THE WORK OF PREPARATION

For the Sufi, spiritual life is a love affair, and from this love affair a child is conceived and then born. This child is the path and also the goal. The eyes of the child are His eyes. The heart of the child beats in harmony with His heart.

For so long He has been waiting. Slowly we come to Him. He awakens the memory of when we were together with Him, and then, through the hard work of aspiration, we prepare a place for our reunion. Through discipline and devotion we learn to meditate, to still the mind and tune into the heart. The practice of meditation energizes the psyche, bringing our shadow to the surface, forcing us to confront our own darkness. Slowly we work upon ourself, clearing away our conditioning, freeing ourself from the desires of the ego.

During this stage of active preparation many people have dreams of cleaning, emptying the house of their psyche of the debris that has gathered since their childhood. One friend dreamt:

> I am very small and am inside myself. I have a shovel and am clearing up all sorts of rubbish. I then find that there is more space for me and I can stretch.

Spiritual life begins with getting down into the muck and mud of the unconscious and working there to integrate and clear it up. So often we cramp ourself into corners, limit our creativity with clutter. We need to make space for ourself to discover the deeper and more dynamic dimension of our inner being. As we slowly empty ourself of rubbish so sunlight begins to stream in. We see and feel the inner landscape of the soul and we become alive there. This is often experienced in dreams in which we find ourself in beautiful gardens, or see radiant cities in luminous landscapes. Frequently these dreams have the quality of being "more real than real life," because the dreamer has touched the eternal dimension of himself.

As we enter this sacred inner world our soul sings to the Beloved, telling Him that we are ready. We have prepared the place for the sacrifice of our self: "Come! How much for a kiss from those precious rubies? If a kiss costs a life, it still must be bought."[2]

It is here, in the secret recesses of the heart, that the relationship with the Beloved takes place. He was always here, waiting to be born into consciousness. But we need to prepare ourself for this meeting, we need to align ourself to the inner vibrations of the Self. How can you notice your invisible lover when your consciousness is filled with the outer world? How can you enter the sacred space of your own heart wearing boots muddied with the desires of the ego? Here lies the esoteric meaning of the immaculate conception. For the Beloved to be conceived as a living presence we need to go through a process of inner purification.

This purification is also a process of rooting ourself in the depths of our own being. Inner work takes us deeper and deeper until we reach the bedrock of our own psyche. It is only when we are standing on the eternally solid ground of the Self that we can come into

His presence without being made totally unbalanced by this dynamic experience. The Beloved belongs to such a different reality from the reality of the ego that our ordinary consciousness cannot begin to comprehend this experience. Grasping anxiously at His limitless void the ego and the mind are thrown into such a confusion that without this inner point of balance the individual can end up in an asylum.

I once had a small experience of the ego's loss of balance in the face of this void. I spent a whole day with my teacher as I had to accompany her to a friend's wedding. Soon after I had taken her back to her apartment I found myself in an electronics shop buying a computer, which I realized when I arrived home I neither wanted or needed. As I looked back at the incident I saw that because my teacher is merged into the nothingness, sitting beside her had been like sitting beside a vast, limitless emptiness. My ego, terrified and threatened by this emptiness, had rushed me off to the store to try and fill it. Luckily I was able to return the computer before even taking it out of its box.

But there are those who have glimpsed this inner dimension without the support of a teacher or the preparation of inner work. The dynamic energy of the beyond can so explode ordinary consciousness that they become unbalanced. I once met a woman who had experienced the tremendous oneness of life in which even the dog's shit on the sidewalk was divine. But she could not contain this experience. As a result she was diagnosed by orthodox medicine as manic-depressive and conditioned by her doctors into believing this. This resulted in her repressing her inner experiences with anti-depressants. Sadly, there are probably many others like her.

SURRENDER AND CONCEPTION

From the moment of *tauba* the wayfarer turns away from the world and begins to surrender his ego consciousness to the greater mystery of the soul. He then encounters the duality of the ego and the Self, a duality which is reflected in the process of negation and affirmation. We say "no" to the ego in order to say "yes" to the Self. Surrender is a highly dynamic state. The "no" contains within it the "yes." It creates a space in which the seed of affirmation can germinate. Through the "no" the "yes" is born. Surrender is thus essentially an act of affirmation. This affirmation, this consent to the Self, attracts the grace of the Beloved: "It is the consent that draws down the grace."

The call of the Beloved energizes the Self. The Self is hidden in the very depths of the unconscious; and it is here, in the unconscious, that the processes of transformation begin to take place, protected from the interference of the ego. Only gradually do the effects of this transformation manifest into consciousness. However, the participation of the wayfarer is all-important. This participation takes place through active preparation, work upon oneself and the practice of meditation. But the wayfarer also participates through surrender, surrendering himself to the energy of the Self. Human beings have free will, and the act of conscious surrender to the higher destiny of the soul is of immense importance. It is essentially accepting the painful process of crucifixion through which the ego is transcended. It is allowing oneself to be made empty for His sake:

> May God empty my very self
> Of all except His own presence. [3]

This act of surrender is the highest offering a human being can make. Then the Beloved cannot help but hold us securely in His heart.

We are made empty and immaculate so that the mystery of His incarnation can take place. Psychologically, we surrender our identification with the ego and bond ourself with the Self. When this bond is strong enough we can contain His presence. There comes a moment in the destiny of the soul when the human and divine energies interact to begin the process of giving birth to the divine consciousness of the Self. This is the moment of conception.

A woman who had been with our group for a few years had the following dream, which describes this happening:

> I am with a few people around a circle of large cubic rocks. In the circle is a lovely little girl of three or four years old. She is sleeping with real abandon lying on her back. She is wearing a pale blue dress with white details on the upper bodice. There is a bird on her heart doing something with its beak. The little girl gets up and comes to me— her dress is covered with white semen from the bird on her heart. I realize that the bird has impregnated her—made love to her in a non-sexual sort of way. The semen is very white. I brush it up with my hand. It is very sweet-smelling. The smell comes into me. The more I smell it the more I want to smell it. I know that the little girl has been very fortunate to have this bird choose her. It is so rare indeed; birds usually mate with birds. I know how special it all is.
>
> The little girl can't go with that wet dress. So I take it off and let it dry a little. Then I put it on her

again and tell her this is her secret.

I wake up because the smell inside me is so
exquisite.

The dream begins with the image of a circle of large
cubic rocks symbolizing the foundations of the dreamer's
psyche. There, in the center of this mandala lies a lovely
little girl. She is dressed in a blue dress with white
brocade. Blue is the color of devotion and the feminine.
It is the color of the Virgin Mary. White symbolizes
innocence and purity. The girl lies sleeping with the
abandonment of innocence and the bird of the spirit is
impregnating her heart. This is the mystery of the
immaculate conception that is taking place in the sacred
place hidden deep within the dreamer's own heart. The
girl is her own pure feminine self whose state of "real
abandon" is in itself an offering to the Beloved.

There is a passage in Rûmî's *Mathnawî* that tells the
story of an idle man who kept praying to God to provide
for him and, to everyone's dismay, his prayers were
answered. Eva de Vitray-Meyerovitch explains the meaning of this story:

> What Rûmî calls idleness, one might better call
> passivity. There is something infinitely passive,
> *totally abandoned, in the heart of the mystic*
> *which calls for God's grace.* It is a kind of virginity
> of the soul comparable to that of Mary in front of
> the Angel of Annunciation. Let us read the com-
> mentary of Ishmael of Ankara:
> "When God's Word enters someone's heart
> and when the divine inspiration fills his heart and
> soul, it is in its nature to produce in him a spiritual
> child having the spirit of Jesus who resuscitates
> the dead."[4]

In the dream the girl is sleeping, suggesting that this state of abandonment is an unconscious state of surrender and trust in the Beloved. Deep within the dreamer, hidden from the doubts of her conscious mind, is an emptiness of intention that relies only on the grace of God. It is this passive purity that has attracted the bird to enact the miracle of impregnation.

The dreamer knows how rare this act is, because "birds usually mate with birds." This means that certain spiritual energies rarely directly interact with human beings, for, as T. S. Eliot wisely remarked, "human kind cannot bear very much reality."[5] There must be an inner purity, an emptiness of surrender, for the higher energies to be able to manifest without destroying the human being. One has to have a central core of trust, a bond with the Beloved, in order to contain the insecurity of a life of the spirit. The ego needs the Higher Self in order to drown itself in safety.

For those who belong to the Beloved this bond was there before the beginning of time. But through his aspirations, meditation, inner-work and surrender the seeker integrates this bond into his human psychic structure—it becomes part of the blood. When this preliminary work has been done the wayfarer is then able to be impregnated by the Beloved—to carry the seed of His consciousness. However, in the dream it is stressed that the bird "chose her." The Beloved chooses His lovers, and "Many are called but few are chosen."[6] In 'Attâr's story of the quest, *The Conference of the Birds*, of all the hundreds of birds who set out on the journey only thirty arrived. How many of those who are attracted to a spiritual path commit their whole self and their whole lifetime to this work?

He calls us to Him. He tests us with many diversions and difficulties. Only when He sees that we are serious, that we are prepared to pay the price, does He unveil Himself in our heart. The Sufi teacher, enacting His will, may also test the wayfarer to the limit: "In a subtle way the Master will put one against himself and then puts the Disciple under a severe test. And if he accepts it, thinking that he cannot do more but die, then he is ready for a high state."[7]

We make every effort and even then it is only because He chooses us that we come to Him. This is the essence of surrender: that all our efforts are valueless and only His grace can help us. Rûmî, speaking in the voice of God, says:

> You imagined that you would accomplish this task through your own strength, activity and effort. This is the wont that I have established: expend everything you have in Our way. Then Our bounty will come to you. In this endless road, We command you to travel with your own feeble hands and feet. We know that you cannot traverse this way with feet so feeble. Indeed, in a hundred thousand years you will not arrive at the first way station. However, when you travel this road until your legs are exhausted and you fall down flat, until you have no more strength to move forward, then God's grace will take you in its arms.[8]

Whatever we do we come to the point where we realize that it is nothing. One friend meditated and worked hard upon herself for years. But then to her deep distress she found that she could not meditate. She could not aspire. This painful situation lasted for some time until suddenly one day she found Him in her heart. He had come so unexpectedly, like "a thief in the night,"[9] and she felt so undeserving. He comes because He wills and it is always more than we could ever expect. And so often we feel, "Why me? What have I done to deserve such sweetness?"

SPINNING THE HEART

In the dream the bird is doing something with its beak to the girl's heart. It is in the heart that the mystery of spiritual conception takes place. This is not the physical heart but what the Sufis call the heart of hearts. The heart of hearts is the heart of the Self which is on the right side of the physical body. In the moment of spiritual conception a special energy is infused into this heart which makes it spin in a particular way. I once had a vision in which my heart was cut open with a knife, taken out and breathed upon—the dust was blown off—and then spun. My teacher did not interpret this inner happening but said that I would come to understand it. Years later I heard her say to someone else that once the heart has been spun in this way it remains spinning for the rest of that person's incarnation.

The divine energy of the Self vibrates at a higher frequency to our ordinary human self. Through the spinning of the heart, the higher consciousness of the Self is able to be integrated into the lower vehicles, into the denser dimensions of the human being. All the wayfarer's spiritual work has been a preparation for this moment, and from now on the work will be to give birth to this seed of consciousness, to attune one's waking consciousness to the higher vibrations of the Self that are now spinning within the heart. This is the gradual process of awakening to the consciousness of the heart, opening the eye of the heart through which the Beloved is able to experience His creation.

Sufis are known as "a brotherhood of migrants who 'keep watch' on the world and for the world,"[10] because through the open eye of His lovers' hearts the Beloved keeps watch on the world. Through His lovers' hearts humanity is kept attuned to the Beloved.

Just as a single heart is spun when the individual is ready to contain the higher energy of the Self, so does this same process happen with a group. When the group has a central core bonded together in love then its collective heart, its central core of light, is spun. In order to help this process, groups of souls that have been bonded together in past lifetimes are forming specific groups. They hold the spiritual core of the group that allows many others to be included in this dynamic unfolding.

The spinning hearts of the lovers of God are forming the map made of points of light which I referred to in the previous chapter. At this time His lovers are being positioned around the planet. Some have already been positioned. Some are moving to physical locations while others are having their hearts awakened to this hidden purpose. Slowly this map is being unfolded, and in certain important places lovers are forming clusters of points of light. Certain spiritual groups have been formed or are being formed to contain these clusters as dynamic centers of light.

When this map of light around the world is fully unfolded it will be able to contain and transform the energy structure of the planet. It has the potential to be the bond that will enable the world soul, the *anima mundi*, to be impregnated with a higher consciousness. The hearts of His lovers form part of the hidden heart of the world. As this map is unfolding so their spinning hearts can open the heart of the world. At this moment in cosmic time the planet is being aligned with its inner source, allowing the world to be infused with a certain cosmic energy that can dramatically speed up the evolution of this planet. If the heart of the world opens, it can receive this frequency of cosmic energy and directly implant it into the hearts of people. This would alter human life more than we could imagine. It is to help in this opening of the heart that many old souls have incarnated at this particular time and are working together.

THE SWEET SMELL OF THE BELOVED

As the heart of the wayfarer turns to the Beloved so the heart of the world turns. Silently we each bring the scent of love into the marketplace of our ordinary lives where it touches the hearts of others. Unknowingly those around us are awakened to the joy that has been missing from life. For too long life has been without the scent of the sacred. When this returns to our city streets it will draw people to the garden of their own soul, and a deep hunger will begin to be satisfied:

> When the fragrance of the I am He is upon the wind,
> The bee of the heart finds the flower of its choice,
> And nestles there, caring for no other thing.[11]

In the dream of the girl and the bird the first impression that the dreamer has of her heart's impregnation is the smell of the bird's semen—"It is very sweet smelling. The smell comes into me. The more I smell it the more I want to smell it." Smell is symbolically the highest sense because it has to do with essence—for example, we speak of a scent being "the essence of roses." A smell conveys something invisible, intangible. In this dream the essence of the dreamer's own divinity comes to her, her own invisible link with the Beloved. Once we have smelled this essence we only want more. It awakens the memory of when we lived in His garden: "A sweet smell has the dust at the feet of my Guru; never I cried before, but now there is no end of sorrow for me. . . . "[12]

SILENCE AND THE SOUL

In the Qur'an we are told that it is Mary's holy silence in the temple that allowed her to conceive the divine Word.[13] In this dream the dreamer tells the little girl that this experience is "her secret." Experiences of the soul need to be kept sacred, and silence is the greatest protection against the pollution of the ego and the disbelief of the world. Silence gives space for the sacred to unfold. Through silence the soul can slowly manifest and share its secrets. If we inwardly rest in silence we are contained in its tenderness and are able to open ourself to life without becoming distorted. Through an inner attitude of silence we can learn to see through the confusion of the outer world and stay true to the essence. Silence has the quality of clarity.

Through silence we can learn to listen to the inner rhythm of our own soul and thus live in harmony with it. As much as we have denied the inner reality of the soul, so we have forgotten the wisdom of silence. We have even grown frightened of silence because it speaks to the emptiness of our material values. When I see people jogging with Walkmans I wonder at their relationship to sound. Is it a necessary distraction from a silence that resonates with some dark secret?

I said to my soul, be still, and let the dark come
upon you
Which shall be the darkness of God. As, in a
theatre,
The lights are extinguished, for the scene to be
changed
With a hollow rumble of wings, with a movement of darkness on darkness,
And we know that the hills and the trees, the
distant panorama
And the bold imposing facade are all being
rolled away—
Or as, when an underground train, in the tube,
stops too long between stations
And the conversation rises and slowly fades
into silence
And you see behind every face the mental
emptiness deepen
Leaving only the growing terror of nothing to
think about;[14]

We need to reclaim silence from the shadow of our
Western culture because silence is the gateway to the
Beloved. Through silence He speaks to us. It is in the
silent spaces of our lives that He comes closest to us. This
is because silence is undefined and He speaks to us of the
endless vistas of our own being. The Beloved cannot be
contained in words, but He can be communed with in
silence. It is for this reason that the deepest prayer is
without words. It is a silent communion within the heart,
a lover's meeting in which words would be a blasphemy.

But silence does not necessarily mean the exclusion
of sound. In our world of opposites we have separated
the two and denied their dialogue. In music we know the
value of the silence between the notes, which, like the

spaces in a Chinese landscape painting, allow a depth of meaning to become manifest. The spaces between sounds speak to us in the same way that the spaces between the stars call us into the beyond. Silence is deeper than sound. "In the beginning was the Word," but silence was before the beginning. Silence is the unmanifest and as such it reminds us of what we were before we experienced separation. The mystic longs to return to this primal state, to "the dark silence in which all lovers lose themselves."[15]

As we become rooted in our own being so we carry this silence beneath the sounds of our everyday life. To be "in the world but not of the world" is to be inwardly immersed in silence and yet at the same time responsive to the sounds of the world. What this means is that we listen to the world with the silent ear of the Beloved. Spiritual conception begins the process of opening our inner ear and becoming attuned to His song which is always present in the silence that underlies creation. We become empty so that we can hear His song for Him.

At the present time this song has a new note. Silence is calling to us, telling us to listen as the hidden name of God becomes manifest amidst the noise of our city streets. Silence comes to us unexpectedly and we no longer need to retire to the mountain to find it. Silence is looking for us with the urgency of a lover. Silence needs to speak to us. It has something to share. The heart of the world is being opened and we need to be present. As with the Virgin Mary it is our own holy silence that will help this spiritual conception to take place. In silence the Beloved is speaking to us, and if we do not listen the moment will pass and many possibilities will be lost. This is a moment of grace that needs to be contained in silence, the silence of a conscious listening to the mystery of the soul.

The lovers of God need to hold the silence of the world so that the marketplace can be impregnated with love. It is not a silence of seclusion, but of passionate involvement with ordinary life that can help His name to be implanted in the blood. Sufis have always been involved in humanity. But until now they have kept their secret message, their bond with the Beloved, hidden and revealed only to friends. But now there is a need for this bond to be made known in public so that those who need to know its existence can openly look for it and find it.

The inner and outer worlds need to be bonded together, the beyond brought into the offices and the shopping malls. There is an urgency about this for at the present time the world is falling apart. The material world carries the painful shadow of our own separation and the inner world haunts us with drug, alcohol and other addictions. The momentum that drove us to dominate the physical world has lost meaning and purpose and become a dangerous addiction in itself. Without the stability of the soul the world can easily disintegrate into total chaos. This moment of transition has its danger.

The opposites of the inner and outer world have become highly polarized. When this happens the tension between the opposites can be either very creative or very destructive. The energy generated by this polarization can either catapult humanity into a new level of awareness or tear the world apart. The bond between the lover and the Beloved is the strongest link with the beyond, and it is through this link that grace can flow into the world. This bond can contain the tension of opposites and allow His grace to catalyze the dynamic of transformation. But for this to happen it must be consciously present in the midst of the outer world. It must be in the marketplace. If it is not totally present then the energy that could create a transformation will only cause further separation between the opposites.

SILENCE AND HOPE

The process of *separatio* has reached a collective ex-
treme. The *coniunctio* of these opposites is not an
abstract ideal but a practical necessity. This union is
already dynamically present in the collective unconscious, manifesting in the leading edge of our Western
consciousness. Sub-atomic physicists see the interplay of
spirit and matter in the dance of the atoms, while the
astronauts' sight of the world as a single living organism
gives us for the first time a visual experience of our
planetary wholeness. The knowledge of the union that
underlies the multiplicity of life has, until now, been held
in secret trust by the mystic. Everything that is created
knows unconsciously this essential oneness:

> And in everything there is a witness for Him
> that points to the fact that He is One.[16]

But the mystic has been the guardian of the *conscious*
knowledge that "Everything is He" (*hama ûst*). It is now
time for this knowledge to be shared more openly.

Our Western culture has become identified with
form, as is evident in the way we value ourselves by what
we do rather than the quality of our experience. We value
our material surroundings more than the inner life which
they contain. Similarly we have identified communication with sound and lost touch with the deeper communion of silence. Those who have attended meditation
meetings or other silent gatherings can attest to the
power of silence and how it allows a quality of communication beyond the range of sound. It is in silence that
hearts speak to each other. Through silence we can
recognize the frequency of souls and the patterns of their
unfolding. In silence there is space for something deeper

than the ego to communicate. For centuries we have learnt how to share words and sounds. Now we need to learn how to share silence. We need to listen to the pulse of our heart and share its hidden purpose with others.

The heart knows the meaning of union, because in essence union is a lovers' meeting. It is this secret dimension of unity that His lovers have held in trust for the world. Through their hearts this consciousness needs to be implanted as a seed into the present stage of global transition. It needs to become part of the collective consciousness of mankind. The silence that underlies our collective chatter—the continual noise of our radios and televisions—instead of carrying the fear of desolation needs to beckon us with the heart's affirmation of love.

If the inner and outer worlds can meet together and be held with the certainty of love then this present transition will lead to a flowering of the world's soul. In the center of the world His lovers need to stand as pillars of hope, for they know the meaning of union. Their hope will counterbalance the fear of the collective, which has become so identified with the outer world that the idea of union with the inner world evokes the terror of the unknown combined with the darkness of the shadow. Fear contracts us into the ego, while hope opens us to the soul. Fear emphasizes the polarization, while hope binds us together. Hope gives space for the future to unfold.

In the silence of the heart hope speaks with the strength of love's certainty. It opens others to the strength of their own need for the beyond. Hope contains the darkness and the insecurity, giving space for His grace to permeate our lives. If we allow it, this world can be a meeting place with the Beloved. His scent can permeate every corner of our lives; the fragrance of our own soul can be found in our most mundane activities. His lovers know this. They have been awakened to the knowledge that "God is All in All;" to quote Mechtild of Magdeburg: "The day of my spiritual awakening was the day I saw and knew I saw all things in God and God in all things."[17]

Spiritual conception is the moment this divine consciousness is implanted within the psyche. In their own inner work seekers prepare the space for this conception, and then they protect this seed until it flowers into consciousness. This solitary work has a direct influence on the world. At this moment the network of lovers who work upon themselves is also preparing the world soul for a possible conception. As individuals and especially as groups they are channeling the grace that can start the heart of the world spinning.

MEETING WITH THE BELOVED IN MEDITATION

But the focus of the seeker always remains upon his or her inner-work. It is only through being empty that space is created for the Beloved to be present; to quote Angelus Silesius:

> God, whose love and joy
> > are present everywhere,
> can't come to visit you
> > unless you aren't there.[18]

If we focus on our relationship with Him, then if it is His will He will turn the heart of the world. The work of the lover is to remain true to the Beloved. In the silence of our hearts we listen to what He wants. This is why meditation is so important, and in the Sufi meditation of the heart we use the energy of love to still the mind and the ego and grasp the hint of the Beloved.[19]

Meditation creates a space for our relationship with the Beloved to become an inner reality. During meditation one friend heard a voice saying, "Meditate." Then over the next two years he had a series of dreams in which he found new rooms in his house. Finally he had a dream in which there was a festival for putting the roof on a new house. Then, during meditation he heard a voice saying, "Hello."

Through meditation we learn to go beyond the mind, into the heart. In the heart lives the Self, "That Person, no bigger than a thumb, burning like flame without smoke, maker of past and future, the same today and tomorrow."[20] The Self is our divine consciousness, the part that knows it is not separate from God. It is eternally present within us, and yet through meditation and aspiration we create a sacred space within the psyche where we can meet. This is the house of God that we slowly build within our ordinary self so that we can make a conscious relationship with our own divinity, not as an abstract ideal, but as a living reality that relates to us.

> If in your heart you make
> a manger for his birth,
> then God will once again
> become a child on earth.[21]

The mystery of His incarnation is always an act of grace, for He chooses us. But through disciplined meditation we attune the mind and the psyche and learn to enter the waiting room of the heart. Through diligence and devotion we learn to listen for Him, so that when He calls us we can respond; when He opens the door of His secret chamber we are there, on the threshold.

Through meditation we look within to where His light is waiting, there, in the very root of our being: "You guard the treasury of God's light—so come, return to the root of the root of your own self."[22] When our ordinary consciousness glimpses this light it adds its own little radiance to His divinity. Then begins the real mystical journey as our consciousness is absorbed deeper and deeper into the dazzling darkness of His light.

He called us and we have come back to Him. We have surrendered our spark of consciousness. This spark of consciousness is His greatest gift, given to mankind for the sake of incarnation. So many evils are done with this spark of consciousness—animals are never so cruel to each other—and it is the greatest act of surrender to offer it back. This surrender is the essence of witnessing, for through our eyes He can now see Himself. We participate in His self-witnessing. Through our surrendering our consciousness He can come to know Himself more fully and thus we are allowed to participate in the prime purpose of creation: "I was a hidden treasure and I desired to be known, therefore I created the world."

In meditation we surrender our consciousness into unknowing. Through the Sufi meditation of the heart we still the mind and then begin to have experiences of *dhyana* in which the individual mind is thrown into the universal mind. For the wayfarer this is experienced as a state of unconsciousness which at first can be mistaken as sleep. But there is an inner wakefulness, a state of being that is a prelude to the higher consciousness of *samadhi* when we awake on another plane of existence. It is then that we know what we were before we were. We experience the wholeness of our natural self.

Yet it is not the ego that has these experiences; through its absence we are present. The surrender of our own individual consciousness allows His consciousness

to be present within us. It is only through His consciousness that we can experience Him. It is only in the light of
the Self that we can perceive the Self; to quote Psalm 36,
verse 9: "In thy light shall we see light." The Blessed John
Ruysbroeck describes this experience: "Here there is
nothing but an eternal seeing and staring at that Light, by
that Light, and in that Light." And he stresses that it is
always an act of grace:

> And to it none can attain through knowledge
> or subtlety, neither through any exercise whatso-
> ever. Only he whom it please God to be united in
> His Spirit, and whom it pleases to enlighten by
> Himself, can see God, and no one else.[23]

The union of individual consciousness with the
Beloved cannot be understood on the level of the mind.
We are thrown beyond the boundaries of our own
understanding into the dark void of His emptiness. It
takes many years to begin to integrate such experiences
into our waking consciousness, to consciously know
what we have experienced. The mind disappears somewhere, and we awaken from meditation not knowing if
minutes or hours have passed. In that dimension there is
no time and no sense of separation. When we return the
light of the beyond shines in our eyes and a knowledge
of nearness is in the heart.

A LINK IN THE CHAIN OF LOVERS

Little by little the ego surrenders, creating space for the
Beloved to enter our life. Instead of the darkness of our
doubts there is a joy, the presence of something we
cannot explain. It remains vague for a long time. It is as

if from time to time we get a refreshing breeze from a distant mountain summit, a little breeze that brings the fragrance of flowers from somewhere else. Slowly our old patterns drop away, and instead an empty, neutral space opens within us in which our higher nature can embody itself.

Unknowingly we begin to see with His eyes. Because the ego is absent we do not know what is happening; only slowly do we become aware that our perception has been changed. We begin to feel this sense of presence, as if someone or something is there behind the visible world. Wordsworth describes this in *Tintern Abbey* :

> And I have felt
> A presence that disturbs me with the joy
> Of elevated thoughts; a sense sublime
> Of something far more deeply interfused,
> Whose dwelling is the light of setting suns,
> And the round ocean and the living air,
> And the blue sky, and in the mind of man:
> A motion and a spirit, that impels
> All thinking things, all objects of all thought,
> And rolls through all things.

For Wordsworth it was in "the meadows and the woods and mountains" that he glimpsed this eternal presence. Nature is beloved by the Sufi because in its beauty His presence is often most easily visible. But He can be felt in so many different ways: as an unexpected closeness to others, or as an inner song which we hear as we walk. He can be· experienced as an invisible wind that blows behind the world, or a joy or peace that creeps upon us unawares. He can be just a sense of being present in the moment without a feeling of time. As we are each unique, so will we perceive Him within His creation in our own unique way.

He will come close to us in the least expected way, because that is the path of least resistance. He who is everywhere usually comes through the back door. Where we do not expect Him, He will be present. What we had sensed in meditation slowly enters into our world. For some it may be a dramatic experience, a revelation. But for most wayfarers it is a gradual opening. Just as the heart slowly opens when we are alone in silence, so does the heart of the world slowly open to us, allowing us to feel Him everywhere.

As we merge into the Beloved, so this world merges into the beyond. We begin to sense the underlying unity of life and flow into that unity. Our life returns to the source where everything is close to Him and in that closeness is made complete—in the words of Meister Eckhart: "Everything is full and pure at its source and precisely there, not outside."[24] Standing in the center of our own being we stand in the central core of the world. We form part of the axis of love, a link in the chain of lovers that helps to hold the world together.

In the present period of transition this chain of lovers is being energized; the axis of love is spinning faster than ever before. A particular vibration of closeness and intimacy is needed to balance the dissolution of the old patterns. People need to be held together with the energy of love to allow old ego attachments to be lost. This is the work of His lovers in the coming years.

Small communities of lovers can contain this quality of intimacy and allow its seeds to germinate in the hearts of others. Just as meditation creates a sacred inner space for the lover to meet the Beloved, so can a community of lovers create a collective space that facilitates this inner relationship for those who come and share in their group meetings. While many groups tend to deny the individual in favor of the collective, lovers know that it is only one's own individual relationship with the Beloved that has any substance. Because the intimacy within the group is born from this individual relationship, it allows individuality to flourish.

In our Naqshbandi group meetings we meditate, drink tea and discuss dreams. The lack of outer form or collective ritual (music or the chanting of the *dhikr*) emphasizes the individual inner journey. The importance given to dreamwork also focuses on the individuality of this journey. No two dreams are the same. Each person's dream poignantly illustrates the singularity of his or her own path, which the dreamer is able to value through sharing the dream. Furthermore, the attention given by the group to the dream, whether verbally through offering an interpretation, or silently through listening, gives a collective appreciation of the dreamer's unique relationship with the beyond.

Within the many different dreams similar threads become apparent. The basic stages of the path which all wayfarers traverse are a visible foundation to the individuality of each person's experience. The dreams offered in this book are an illustration of this. In this chapter the same process of spiritual conception is portrayed with very different imagery: the little girl impregnated by the bird has a symbolic richness in total contrast to the bare factuality of the house being prepared for the presence of the Beloved. Yet in both dreams the same ancient journey is seen unfolding in the heart and psyche of the wayfarer. This sense of a shared inner destiny of the heart helps create the intimacy and quality of belonging that is so important to the well-being of the group. In our innermost moments as well as in times of desolation we each know that the journey is the "flight of the alone to the Alone." But the bond of the group helps to contain this terrible aloneness of the quest. It helps us to walk our own individual, lonely path amidst the collective pressures of the world.

In the previous chapter I mentioned how the group can be bonded outside of time, because they belonged together with the Beloved before creation. In the group this bond manifests in the shared journey home. Wayfarers who were together in union share their experience of separation, and individually they walk the same path back to the Beloved. Thus the group embraces the whole spiritual journey of union, separation and then union as an inner foundation, as a collective imprint in the heart. In the group meetings, through the sharing of silence and dreams, and just being together, drinking tea and talking, this imprint becomes integrated into consciousness. It becomes part and parcel of our daily life, not just spoken but inwardly understood. This primal song of the soul is able to permeate our outer lives, and resonate in the marketplace, where although inaudible to the outer ear, it is there for those who need it.

This song attracts the attention of seekers for whom the bond with the Beloved is not so strong and who lack the inner certainty of their own spiritual convictions. The core of the group is able to contain these seekers, and include them within the sheltering arms of their own sense of belonging. This security allows these seekers to open to their own intimate self, a process which often evokes feelings of great vulnerability.

The core group of bonded lovers is like a tree providing shelter for those in need. This tree is rooted in the hearts of His lovers and is thus nourished directly by the Beloved. It stands at the axis of the world, in the stream of His love. Within the group this stream of love manifests as the tradition of the path, which is a particular flow of energy that takes the wayfarer home. Naqshbandi Sufis are known as golden Sufis because the energy of this tradition has a golden yellow color. The musical note of this line is D.

THE TEACHER AND THE GROUP

At the center of this tree is the teacher, who is the living guardian of the energy of the path as it comes into the world. Within the heart of the teacher the tradition is held as an uninterrupted line of succession stretching back through his or her teacher and the chain of superiors. It is through this chain of transmission that the energy of the tradition manifests. If the teacher and the group do not stay within the tradition then the energy ceases to flow. This means that a certain unwritten code of behavior and inner attitude need to be followed, and it is the responsibility of the teacher to keep the group within these principles. Irina Tweedie describes this:

> Meditation, spiritual life, without the highest ethics is impossible. In this tradition we put great emphasis on ethics. In our group, when I see that someone doesn't live as they should they are asked to leave. Sometimes that helps. Usually they come back because they understand and make the necessary changes. But sometimes one must give the person this push. I don't like to do it. I don't do it for my pleasure. I tell the person once. I tell them twice or I say, "You cannot do this. It is not honest. It is not decent. You are disturbing the others and you are hurting them." Then if they still don't understand I have to say, "Leave! This place is not for you."[25]

The teacher is also the most visible outer focus for the wayfarer. Often when we first come to a spiritual group our inner bond with the Beloved is not yet known. It is experienced as longing, discontent, an inability to fit into the outer world. It may take years of painful unveiling to discover the security of this ultimate belonging. The bond of fellow travelers helps to hold us until we find this real security. But the relationship with the teacher is usually the most powerful reminder and container of our bond with the Beloved.[26] Furthermore, for many wayfarers it is through their relationship with the teacher that they first tune into the energy of the path.

On the inner level of the soul the teacher holds the group within his heart. The group is thus bonded to the teacher as a child is bonded to its mother. It is this instinctual bond of the heart that enables the teacher to be responsive to the needs of the group and keep the group aligned with the tradition. It is through this bond of the heart that the teacher comes to know about any disturbances that happen within the group and its members. Irina Tweedie has said that she would come to know about an individual's spiritual difficulties, but that it would be quicker if the person actually told her.

In particular it is the function of the teacher to keep the wayfarer bonded to the path and the whole group bonded together within the energy stream of the tradition. The teacher will not allow anyone to disturb this bond, and at times will have to throw someone out of the group if they cause an inner disturbance or behave in an ethically unacceptable manner. Also, if the collective attitude of the group begins to stray from the highest principles of the path, the teacher may have to shock them, in order to keep them consciously focused and thus in tune with the path. Irina Tweedie would at times seriously threaten to close her group when she sensed

that people were not working hard enough on themselves.

The bond between the teacher and the group is a
bond of love and through this bond the group is both
energized and protected. The more a group meditates
and aspires so the greater the light that it generates. There
are forces in the world which are disturbed by this light
and who would like to interfere with the work of the
group. The teacher, merged within his teacher, merged
within a great succession of the friends of God, protects
the group from any such interference. It is the state of
surrender of the teacher that enables the grace of the
succession of the friends of God to hold the group in the
heart of God. In this way the aspirations of His lovers and
their work in the world are protected by the succession
of the friends of God who watch over mankind.

It is not necessary for the teacher to be physically
present in the group for this inner bond to function. It is
on the level of the soul that the process of belonging and
protection takes place. The hearts of the lovers who form
the core of the group are bonded together as a group soul
that spins with the energy of love. The Higher Self of the
teacher watches over this dynamic unfolding. Occasion-
ally it may be necessary for the teacher to be physically
present in order to keep the attention of the group
attuned to the path, and not allow the inner bond to be
compromised by personality conflicts or other misunderstandings. In the same way the outer teacher at times
needs to help an individual stay focused on the goal.

In the coming age, spiritual groups will function
more and more as living organisms generating love and
light. The teacher will become a less dominant physical
presence and the group will become more responsible
for itself. The attitude of a group being "spoon-fed" by the
teacher, totally dependent upon his presence, will inter-

fere with the energy flow of the tradition as it comes into the world. Inwardly the teacher will always be the custodian of the group, but it is the dynamic of the group that will create a sacred space for those who wish to come closer to themselves. It is the ordinary members of the group who will form the pillars of the temples of the future; and the bond of spiritual friendship found within a group will become increasingly important. To be a part of such a group is a blessing.

Inwardly the teacher is the closest friend of the wayfarer and this relationship resonates with the intimacy that comes only from the merging of souls. But outwardly the relationship with the teacher is often remote. The teacher represents a distant goal, the deepest longing for union. The friendship found within a group of fellow wayfarers helps the seeker to include his ordinary self within the context of the path. The group holds the energy of the outer world more visibly than the teacher and thus the group helps to bridge the gap between the secrets of the heart and everyday life.

The spiritual group is the container for the process of spiritual conception that is now beginning all over the world. In groups of sincere seekers the inner and outer worlds are being bonded together enabling the song of the soul to be heard in the world. Many groups of different spiritual traditions have reincarnated together at this time in order to facilitate this process. Slowly the different groups are being inwardly aligned with each other so that their vibrations do not interfere but complement each other. This is not a visible or conscious process, but it is directed by the superiors of the different traditions. It is this unfolding pattern of love that will enable the oneness of the Beloved to surface into the collective consciousness of mankind.

STAGES OF PRAYER

Realization is simply to give birth to something within oneself.
Anonymous

SEPARATION AND NEARNESS

At the beginning the path is hard and stony. The seeker needs to make every effort to stay focused on a goal which appears so distant and inaccessible. He who is so close to us is known only as a "sigh in the soul," a sadness and longing for something invisible. This is the lament of the reed at the beginning of Rûmî's *Mathnawî*:

> Listen to the reed how it tells a tale, complaining of separations,
> Saying, "Ever since I was parted from the reed-bed, my lament has caused man and woman to moan.
> It is only to a bosom torn by severance that I can unfold the pain of love-desire.
> Everyone who is left far from his source wishes back the time when he was united with it."

All pilgrims pass along this road, when our only sense of the Beloved is His absence, and our pain just amplifies

57

our isolation and loneliness. This is the dark night of the soul that is known to every seeker, as Gerard Manley Hopkins voices: "And my lament is cries countless, cries like dead letters sent to him that lives alas! away."[1] Only the fire burning in our heart and the knowledge of those who have walked before us keep us putting one foot in front of the other. It is our desperation that drives us forward.

But gradually the pilgrim and the path begin to change and flowers appear between the hard stones. We slowly sense the closeness of the Beloved. As the veils of separation become thinner so it is His presence rather than His absence that begins to take us home. Before it was the torment of a world without Him that pushed us along; now it is the fondness of His embrace that draws us to Him. The more we come into His presence the greater His grace, and the path that had required every effort becomes effortless: "How can there be an effort with divine things? They are given, infused. . . . "[2]

Saint Teresa of Avila delineates this process of transition as four stages of prayer: recollection, quiet, union and ecstasy. She uses the image of a gardener watering his garden to describe these stages. At the beginning the gardener must make every effort to lift the water from the well, but slowly the effort of the gardener becomes less and less, until in the final stage there is no longer a gardener, only the Lord Himself soaking the garden in abundant rain.

RECOLLECTION

The first stage is the work of keeping one's attention on God despite all the distractions of the world. This is the process of turning away from the world, the negation, in which the inner attention of the seeker is turned away from the outer world and the desires of the ego back towards the Beloved. It is often a time when the seeker is assailed by doubts and difficulties, as the ego and the mind try to obstruct us and convince us of the uselessness of our quest. Why search for something invisible that demands sacrifice and suffering when there are the visible, tangible attractions of this world? The ego knows that death awaits it on the path, and so it will use all its skills to create every possible confusion and problem to deter the seeker. Furthermore, because the ego is the central part of our consciousness it knows where we are most easily led astray. Nothing knows our weaknesses better than our own self. Nothing can distract us more easily than our own mind.

The ego stands firmly between the seeker and the light that is hidden within him. The ego blocks us from the influence, guidance and help that come from the Beloved. It tells us that we are weak and unable to make the journey. Like the birds at the beginning of 'Attâr's *The Conference of the Birds*, it offers innumerable excuses. The nightingale says that he is not strong enough for such a journey, his love for the rose is enough. The duck timidly says that she cannot leave the familiar water to cross the valleys to fly to the Simurgh (the object of the quest), while the partridge is so attached to precious stones that he is not interested in seeking the true jewel. They all say that they do not want to give up their tranquil lives and are too feeble to reach the Sublime Simurgh.

In 'Attâr's fable the Hoopoe, who is the birds' guide, encourages them to love rather than think about themselves:

He who loves does not think about his own
life; to love truly a man must forget about himself,

be he ascetic or libertine. If your desires do not
accord with your spirit, sacrifice them, and you
will come to the end of your journey. If the body
of desire obstructs the way, reject it; then fix your
eyes in front and contemplate.[3]

Love is the desire of the heart that can help us overcome
the desires of the ego. Saint Paul said, "love bears all
things;" love gives us the strength to bear the difficulties,
doubts and uncertainties that the ego and the mind place
in our path. If we identify ourselves as lovers then we
know the meaning of our sacrifice and we can cross the
desert that lies between the ego and the Self.

Love helps us to stay true to the essence of our quest
in these testing times. Yet so often the heart itself seems
barren or closed. Saint Teresa, describing this state, says:
"for days on end one feels nothing but dryness, dislike
and distaste."[4] This is the time for perseverance, when
will-power and determination are needed to see us
through. Pride can also be helpful. Not the pride of the
ego that says I am better than others, but the dignity of
the Self, the instinctual inner nobility of the human being
which speaks to the suffering ego and says, "Others have
done this before me and I am not less than they." The
spiritual path is the most demanding challenge that can
face a human being. But because it is the call of the higher
Self it also evokes our best qualities, including the
archetypal energy of the warrior for whom no challenge
is too great. To quote Rûmî: "In the language of lovers the
word impossible does not exist."

During this testing time the seeker is being carefully
watched by the superiors of the line to see if he is serious.
Does he have the necessary qualities to make this
journey? Can he walk this desert with no encouragement
but the knowledge that there is nowhere to go back

to? The doors of the world have closed slowly behind him; old friends and activities no longer hold any interest.

Yet in this desert we are being prepared. The focus of our whole psyche is being shifted from the ego to the Self. The dryness that we experience is an effect of our ordinary consciousness being disengaged from our inner self as this shift takes place. We still continue to live our outer life but often it seems to have no meaning or purpose, nor does the inner world offer any fulfillment. Meaning comes from our connection to the inner world. Inwardly we are being realigned with the Self and the deepest meaning of the soul. But only when the process is complete can we experience this different level of meaning. In the meantime we suffer the barrenness of being disconnected from the old ego-oriented values and can only trust that this desolation has a higher purpose.

At this time we need to remember that we are lovers and that our life is empty because He is not with us. We show Him our sincerity by faithfully waiting for Him to return. One day when Bhai Sahib saw Irina Tweedie sitting in this state of depression he said to her, "Do not say, 'It will pass.' Because it will pass. Instead, just say to the Beloved, 'Beloved, I am still faithful. I am still true.' Then you turn the tables on God and He cannot help but come to you."[5]

In this first stage, which can last for years, life feels empty because we are being emptied and our attention is being turned towards a world which as yet we cannot see. We are being ground down until we are thin enough to pass through the narrow door that opens into the spiritual dimension of our own being.

QUIET

Our effort of recollection, our focus on the beyond and our disciplined practice of meditation make up the thread that guides us across these barren days. Then slowly, imperceptibly, the scene begins to change. As we walk towards Him, often going one step backwards for every two we go forward, He comes to meet us. And for every step we make towards Him He makes ten towards us. At first we do not know this, so great is the apparent distance between us. But one day we realize that the desolation is no longer there. There is a sense of peace that has arrived unnoticed; the wind is not bitter and cold but soft. Irina Tweedie describes how it happened to her:

> And so it came. . . . It tiptoed itself into my heart, silently, imperceptibly, and I looked at it with wonder. It was a still, small, light-blue flame, trembling softly. It had the infinite sweetness of a first love, like an offering of fragrant flowers with gentle hands, the heart full of stillness and wonder and peace.[6]

He who we thought had betrayed us, whom we had doubted and despaired of, comes to us when we are ready. Without our knowing it the dryness of the desert has opened us. We have shown Him that as lovers we were prepared to endure deprivation; that we would not return to the world just because He seemed to have abandoned us. He had called us to Him and then left us in the dark night of our own despair. We cried out, like Hopkins, "No worst, there is none. . . . Comforter, where is your comforting? Mary, mother of us, where is your relief?"[7] Each of our cries reached Him, but He had to wait until we were desperate enough. As a friend was told in a dream, "You must reach the point of total despair." Because only then does the cry of the lover come from the very depths of the soul, and the grip of the ego is shattered by the need of the heart:

> You'll be free from the trap of your being,
> when, through spiritual need,
> You're trodden underfoot, like a mat,
> in the mosque and the wine house.[8]

Yet this experience of desolation and transformation is not a single happening but a process that is repeated many times over as the ego gradually loses its hold. Slowly we die to the world and each death is painful. But as the ego holds our attention less there is more space for the Beloved and for His servant, the Self. Each time after a period of darkness it always amazed me how He gave more than I could ever imagine. Each time it becomes somehow easier because we consciously come to know the value of our sacrifice—we know that we suffer in order to come closer to Him. Al-Hallâj so deeply understood the relationship between suffering and the Beloved that he said, "Suffering is He Himself, whereas happiness comes from Him."[9]

In our desolation we suffer His separation from Himself. Then He lifts a veil and gives us a glimpse of our real Self and of the infinite tenderness He has for His lovers. After this our spiritual life changes and we begin to experience His presence rather than only His absence. Once we have glimpsed the luminosity of our real nature we slowly become blind to the attractions of the world. In the brighter light of the Self the ego appears shadowy and insubstantial. We do not reject the world; rather it falls away and we begin to rest in God. Saint Teresa describes this as the second degree of prayer, the prayer of the quiet:

> Now the soul begins to be recollected, and
> here it comes into touch with the supernatural, to
> which it could not possibly attain by its own
> efforts. . . . On arriving at this state, the soul begins
> to lose the desire for earthly things—and no
> wonder! It clearly sees that not even one moment
> of this joy is to be obtained here on earth, and that
> there are no riches, estates, honours, or delights
> that can give it such satisfaction even for the
> twinkling of an eye. For this is the true joy, the
> content that can be seen to satisfy.[10]

At this stage the seeker has begun to surrender to God
and He begins to take over. In Saint Teresa's image of
watering the garden, the gardener, instead of drawing
water manually from the well, now has "a device with a
windlass, and so draws more water with less labour, and
is able to take some rest instead of being continually at
work."[11] Gradually the Beloved does more and more and
we learn to co-operate. We learn to give space to the
Beloved and allow Him to live through us. It is from this
relationship of love that the Self is conceived and then
born.

EFFORT AND GRACE

The transition from effort to grace is a wondrous unfolding. It is particularly unexpected for our Western consciousness which has become almost totally identified
with the ego and the masculine power drive. The goal-
less goal of the Self is a state of being in which everything
is given. Only through our greatest effort can we trans-
cend the ego and yet we cannot do this without grace.
Abu Saîd al-Kharrâz expresses the apparent paradox:

"Whoever believes he can reach God through his own efforts toils in vain; whoever believes he can reach God without effort is merely a traveller on the road of intent."[12]

Slowly our consciousness leaves the prison of the ego and is attuned to the higher frequency of the Self. Edinger describes this shift in awareness:

> As the process deepens one realizes more and more that insights come by grace and that development occurs not by the will of the ego but by urge to development from the Self.[13]

The ego has definable aims and purposes belonging to a tempo-spatial world. But the purposes of the Self cannot be grasped by ordinary consciousness because they belong to a different level of reality. They can be glimpsed in meditation, hinted at in a vision or a dream, but they always point beyond the known into the unknown. The greatest adventure requires that we make every effort to surrender to the unknown and allow ourself to be taken beyond space and time. The Self is a dynamic state of being that opens us to the infinite present.

The following dream images the birth of the Self and how it involves the transition from effort to grace. The dreamer was a man.

> In the first part of the dream I was with an old silver-haired woman whose name was Lady Loveridge. She was my employer or superior in some way. I was wearing a black tie with an emblem of some kind on it. It was similar to a college or university tie. She asked me why I was wearing this tie as I was not entitled or supposed to wear it. I replied that I had found it in my

grandfather's house so I decided to wear it, not realizing that it was not for me to do so. I asked her husband, who was standing behind her, if it was really a bad thing to do and he replied, "No, but you are not really supposed to." It was said to be the tie of those who worked.

In the next part of the dream I was with Lady Loveridge again. This time she was wearing a silk tie of rich blue colors. I put my hand up into the inside of the tie and then when I tried to pull it out I found that it was stuck fast. I was connected fast in some way to the tie.

In the third part of the dream I was to go on a journey and a receptionist named Grace asked me if I had said goodbye to Lady Loveridge. I answered that I had not. Grace then asked me to do so, saying that Lady Loveridge would be upset if I did not, as she was extremely fond of me. I then replied that I had not done so before because I was completely naked. At this point I was wearing a long black overcoat which I opened to show Grace my nakedness. As I looked down I noticed without shame or embarrassment that I had an erection.

In the last part of the dream I was heavily pregnant and Grace said that she was to help in the delivery of the child. The birth however was so very easy, painless, and without labour. After I asked Grace what I had she replied that I had given birth to a beautiful baby girl. At this news I was filled with great joy, bliss almost, and happiness—first that there should be a baby and second that it should be a girl.

The dream begins with the dreamer wearing a black tie which he was told by Lady Loveridge, a silver-haired old woman, that he was not entitled to or supposed to wear. The fact that the dreamer found it in his grandfather's house suggests that it comes from the collective conditioning. The father or mother often symbolizes a dreamer's personal conditioning: the attitudes and complexes impressed upon us by the individual psychological make-up of our parents. Grandparents symbolize the collective, archetypal realm. It is the grandparents who give a child a sense of family history stretching back into the past; and it is often the grandparents who tell the stories, introducing the child to the larger, mythic dimension of the collective.

A tie, like a university or collective tie, gives the wearer a sense of collective identity. In this dream the black tie with an emblem that the dreamer found in his grandfather's house was the tie of "those who worked." This is a powerful collective identity particularly for a man: we belong because we work. It is for this reason that many people who experience unemployment suffer not only material hardship, but also the psychological stress of feeling that they no longer belong—they are no longer a part of the great collective mass of working people. Work has also acquired a moral dimension, particularly since the Victorian era, with the idea that the devil makes mischief for idle hands. This collective conditioning helps humanity to counter a natural inertia and laziness but it is less helpful when it dominates a seeker's attitude to the inner journey.

Effort and hard work are very necessary for the inner process of preparation. But there is also a time to surrender every effort. In the previous chapter I mentioned Rûmî's story of the idle man whose prayers were answered and how this relates to the emptiness or state of abandon that is necessary for the process of spiritual conception. Our dreamer is clearly told that the collective conditioning of effort and work is not appropriate.

CAUGHT IN LOVE'S GRASP

In the next part of the dream, instead of the dreamer wearing a black tie, Lady Loveridge is wearing a blue silk tie. The dreamer, putting his hand into the inside of her tie, is stuck fast, connected in some way to her tie. The dreamer is caught in love's tie of devotion, in the feminine mystery of the Beloved. In the words of 'Attâr:

> My heart on your tresses' twists
> Was caught, not just my heart,
> My soul too, in the same crux
> Became entangled.[14]

Being caught by the Beloved is a feminine mystery because it takes place in the unconscious—we are caught without consciously knowing it. When we fall in love with another human being our unconscious takes us into love's arena and often holds us there, a suffering slave. With the Beloved we know even less of the mystery that binds us. We are taken to Him through the door of the unconscious that every lover leaves open. Another friend had a simple dream in which she had a lasso in her left hand and a razor in her right hand. The right symbolizes consciousness, and in this dream the razor images the path "as narrow as the edge of the razor" which she has to walk with open eyes. This is the conscious act of discrimination which is one of the most important qualities for spiritual life. But the lasso that will capture and bind her is in her left hand, for this will happen in the unconscious depths of her being, where the covenant between the lover and the Beloved was engraved before the beginning of time.

Rûmî tells a sad tale which describes the same theme that the Beloved unexpectedly grasps the lover, never to let him go. He also includes the notion that it is the spiritual need of the lover that precipitates this:

> A schoolteacher who was so utterly destitute that he had only a cotton shirt to wear even on cold winter days was standing by a rushing mountain stream when he suddenly saw a bear in the water. The animal had fallen into the gushing waters high up in the mountains and was now being carried by the torrential waters down to the village. The schoolchildren, pitying their teacher, told him to jump into the water and seize the fine fur coat that had apparently arrived there as a much-appreciated gift. Out of despair he jumped into the water, but the bear, still very much alive, grasped him and drew him close to its body. When the horrified children saw this, they asked the teacher to let the fur coat go, but he answered: "I'll let the fur coat go, but the coat does not let me go!"[15]

"Love is God's trap,"[16] and love is also the noose around the neck of the lover, hanging him till he dies so that the Beloved can live within him: "The Beloved is living, the lover is dead." In love, death and birth are united, for death unites the lover with the Beloved. This death is the annihilation of the "I," one's individual qualities. To quote al-Ghazzâlî: "There is nothing good in love without death."[17] The seeker must surrender every-thing, even every effort, so that love can take him beyond the ego, back to the root of the root of his own self. It is then that the lover's essence can merge with the Beloved.

When we know that we are caught, held fast by love, we have already surrendered and are experiencing this inner connection of love. This connection is a state of union which is as yet unconscious, but is the seed of conception that leads to the birth of the Beloved within the soul of the lover. It is when the Beloved is born that He begins to infuse the lover's consciousness with His knowledge of Himself.

THE SPIRAL DANCE OF DEATH

Slowly the ego dies. Slowly the lover gets absorbed into the Beloved. Slowly His consciousness permeates what is left of the lover. With each little death a veil is torn away and the closeness that had been hidden within the heart becomes more and more part of our everyday life. There are stages on this journey, moments of death and moments of birth, times of transition and times that seem to be empty of progress. But one of the difficulties of trying to describe this journey is that it is not linear. It is not a path from A to B. Rather it is a circumambulation of the soul, a spiral dance that draws us towards the center of ourself where the lover and the Beloved have always been united.

We were together before the beginning of time. We journey towards this point that is always present because it exists outside of time. Within the experience of time it is always an endless journey. Al-Hallâj, the great martyr of love who was executed for exclaiming his annihilation in the famous statement, "*anâ'l-Haqq*" ("I am the Absolute Truth"), danced in his fetters to the gallows because he knew that death would remove the final temporal veil. His last words were "*hasb al-wâjid ifrâd al-wâhid lahu*" ("it is enough for the lover that he should make the One single.")[18] It is this state of oneness imprinted within the lover that draws him ever closer and infuses him with the longing to die. Like al-Hallâj's metaphor of the moth, we spiral to our death attracted by the light of the Beloved that burns within us.

As the lover comes closer to the center of himself that is not separate from the Beloved so the path becomes more and more a state of being. The wayfarer experiences the path as no longer something separate. As the lover gradually dies so does the path gradually disappear. How can there be stages on a path that does not exist? Our experience of separate stages belongs to our experience of separation. This is one of the paradoxes. There are separate stages that appear to follow each other—there are the seven valleys of the quest as 'Attâr outlines in *The Conference of the Birds*—but in the heart there is only the limitless sea of love. Bhai Sahib's response to the notion of spiritual progress was, "Swimming in the infinite ocean who is nearer the shore? We are all beginners of course. . . ."[19]

The lover knows only too well the difference between the desolation of the desert and the bliss of His embrace. Yet in the intensity of any spiritual experience, whether sadness or bliss, there is only the moment. There is no before and no after. In the moments of separation, although the mind may retain memories of closeness, these memories are swamped by the feelings of isolation. When we are touched by His bliss everything else disappears. It is this experience of the atemporal nature of the Self that makes spiritual life so intense.

The birth of the Self is a growing awareness of this atemporal dimension of our being. As we slowly die to the ego so our consciousness gradually shifts. We may speak of annihilation, but one is not annihilated; one cannot disappear. Irina Tweedie explains:

Nothing in nature disappears; it only changes. We do not disappear, we only change a great deal. One does not only have the feeling of liberation but one lives in a completely different world from that of the ordinary mind and senses. . . . It involves a completely new and changed consciousness with a totally different kind of knowledge and a new way of seeing. Later, when this new consciousness completely impresses the senses and the ordinary mind we experience quite unexpected harmony. It comes unexpectedly and changes our life. We see life in a new light, as if made from another material and thus it acquires a new meaning.[20]

As the journey spirals inward so we come closer to experiencing life from this new center of consciousness. We see ourself from different angles. We experience the Beloved reflected in different ways: as beauty and as majesty, as bliss and as pain. But these differences more and more point towards oneness and at the same time grow in intensity. To quote Irina Tweedie again:

All movement on the spiral path. . . can be seen as simultaneous happenings which are only subtle variations in the center. . . . The spiral is an incredibly beautiful symbol. The situations repeat themselves again and again. The nearness to the Beloved grows deeper and deeper. The despair when He veils His face grows greater and greater. Until one day all that disappears somewhere.[21]

The birth of the Self is the integration of opposites that takes place at the center of the spiral.

NAKEDNESS AND INCEST

In the dream with Lady Loveridge and Grace, the dreamer has been caught in love's grasp. He is held in the inner connection that will take him home. Now he must say goodbye to the silver-haired old woman, Lady Loveridge, for he has to discover love's mystery within himself. On this journey towards oneness we leave behind everything that is other than ourself. We follow love's call to "Open your hidden eyes and return to the root of the root of your own self."[22]

This is a moment of inner nakedness in which we become aware that we must go home just as we are; to quote Bhai Sahib: "You come naked into the world and you go naked. When you come to a spiritual teacher you have to be naked."[23] There comes the time for many of us when we dream that we are naked, usually naked in public. Often we are embarrassed in the dream because we have been conditioned to cover ourselves, to be other than what we really are. Once an elegantly dressed woman came to our group. We leave our shoes in the hallway and sometimes Irina Tweedie, seeing that a newcomer may be unaware of this, asks him or her to take off the shoes. Without consciously knowing what she was saying she asked this woman, "Please take off your clothes and come in." The lady never came again.

We have to accept ourself as we are and not as we think we are. It is only as our real self that we can be transformed. When the dreamer reveals his nakedness to Grace he sees that he has an erection, which points to the next stage of his inner journey. The sexual imagery suggests the process of alchemical transformation, imaged in the alchemical proverb: "I looked at myself, I mated with myself, I gestated myself, I gave birth to myself, I am myself."[24] Robert Johnson relates this proverb to the inner meaning of incest, which is the introversion of the energy of consciousness. Through the practice of meditation and inner work, consciousness which normally flows into the outer world is being introduced to the energies that normally flow in the unconscious.

> When you go off to meditate. . . you are mating with yourself. One stream of energy is being introduced to another stream of energy, and their fusion produces an offspring, which, like a physical child, has the characteristics of the two parent energies but is independent and often superordinate to both.[25]

Introversion is the source of all spirituality. When we cannot look inward or the conditions do not allow us to do this, we cannot become renewed. Introversion is the sign of those who have started to take the path seriously and the true mystic needs introversion as much as others need air for breathing. Once we are already on the path we experience that our need for introversion gets stronger, and with this the wish to discover *that* which is hidden within us.

The Self, which is one with God, responds to the call of the Beloved and awakens our heart to the quest. Our heart has reminded us of our real home, and as exiles we begin the journey thither, turning our attention away from the outer world towards our inner being. Through meditation, aspiration and inner work we create a space in our psyche for the Self, allowing it to come into our ordinary consciousness. The Self has been eternally present in the depths of the unconscious, but our conscious work enables it to be integrated into consciousness. Our experience of the Self is born from the interaction of consciousness with the depths of the unconscious. These are the opposites that give birth to the divine child.

However, the Self is not a being but a state of being. In its feminine aspect it is essentially an inner emptiness that allows the divine to be present. It is a state of stillness that allows us to experience the divine stillness. Stillness is both the method and the aim. Through meditation we still the mind and through inner work we integrate our conflicting emotions and other psychological disturbances, creating stillness out of chaos. We calm the body, quiet the desires, perceptions and feelings in order to arrive at the eternal stillness that lies beyond the mind. At first the stillness lasts only for a few seconds, but as we meditate regularly so the stillness lasts longer, until it becomes eternally present, whatever the noise or disturbances of the outer world.

In the silence we can hear the still small voice of the Beloved. The Self is a state of consciousness that is eternally receptive to the Divine Hint.

THE FEMININE MYSTERY OF THE SOUL

In the fourth and final part of the dream the dreamer gives birth—"the reborn is his own begetter." Grace is the midwife, for grace is "the Beloved's nurturing of the lover by His sympathy and supportiveness, so that the lover may attain full strength and vigor in order to behold His beauty."[26] Through this whole process we are contained within His love. It is only through His support and constant companionship that we can become conscious of our own innermost secret.

Grace tells the dreamer that he has given birth to a beautiful baby girl. This news fills the dreamer with "great joy, bliss almost, and happiness—first that there should be a baby and second that it should be a girl." This child is the Self and it is a girl, imaging the state of inner receptivity that is the divine feminine. In mythological imagery she is the pure virgin in whose lap the unicorn will lay its horn. The unicorn's horn symbolizes the masculine spirit of transformation, the energy of the Christ principle. Thus the birth of the Self has a feminine and a masculine aspect. The feminine is the state of inner purity and receptivity that allows the masculine spirit to be incarnated into consciousness.

The feminine and masculine aspects of the Self reflect the relationship of the soul and the Beloved. In the hidden place of the heart the soul opens to the Beloved, as the *Song of Solomon* passionately exclaims:

> I sleep, but my heart waketh: it is the voice of my beloved that knocketh, saying, Open to me my beloved, my sister, my love, my dove, my undefiled: for my head is filled with dew, and my locks with the drops of the night. . . .
>
> I rose up to open to my beloved; and my hands dropped with myrrh, and my fingers with sweet smelling myrrh, upon the handles of the lock.
>
> I opened to my beloved; but my beloved had withdrawn himself, and was gone: my soul failed when he spake: I sought him, but I could not find him; I called him but he gave me no answer.[27]

When the Beloved is present the lover experiences a bliss which often has an erotic quality, and the lover is always the receptive one impregnated by the Beloved. When He is absent our heart waits. In either case the lover's inward attitude is feminine. It is a state of surrender through which the Beloved can enter the lover's heart and life when He will, "a relationship in which the mystical soul

. . . becomes the 'mother of her father' *omm abî-hâ.*"[28]

The lover becomes the bride of the Beloved, belonging only to Him. He is invisible but eternally present, and He tells His bride the secrets of love which are only shared between lovers. In the depths of the heart He tells us all we need to know, not with words but "whispered in the unspeakable but eloquent silence of God."[29] It is to His bride that He reveals His own mystery, because it is this inner feminine attitude of surrender that enables the lover to give birth to the Beloved as a living reality within his own heart.

ATTENTIVENESS IN PRAYER

Now slowly, after all our discipline and work, we become familiar with the empty silence that is in the very core of our being. It is here that the real prayer takes place; a prayer born not from desire but from merging. A prayer in which we are a part of His prayer. The Sufi says that all prayer comes from Him: "I call Thee, no, Thou callest me unto Thee!"[30] In the silent niche of the heart the lover experiences the truth that there is only one prayer that underlies all of creation—the prayer in which He is present, not as a personal God or creator, but as something both inexpressible and intimate. In this innermost recognition of the heart the lover recognizes the Beloved as something inseparable from himself. The lover remembers his primal awareness that there is nothing other than Him. The awareness of the heart is the act of witnessing that is the foundation of all prayer and all praise. In the words of Rûmî:

> Become silent and go by the way of silence
> towards non-existence.
> And when you become non-existent you will

77

be all praise and all laud.[31]

With our heart turned towards the Beloved we realize that we belong to Him and have always belonged to Him. Our work is then to be attentive to Him, which Saint John of the Cross describes as an effortless state:

> [We] must be content with a loving peaceful attentiveness to God, and live without the concern, without the effort, and without the desire to taste or feel Him. All these desires disquiet the soul and distract it from the peaceful quiet and sweet idleness of the contemplation which is being communicated to it.[32]

One can only be fully attentive if one is without desire, even the desire to be with God. Meister Eckhart describes this as true spiritual poverty: "so long as you have any desire to fulfill the will of God and have any hankering after eternity and God, for just so long you are not truly poor."[33] If our attention is to be fully focused on the Beloved we must want nothing for ourselves.

The more we are inwardly attentive to Him the more fully He participates in our daily life. His prayer permeates our life and becomes the foundation of our consciousness. At first we are not aware of His presence and participation in our life, partly because we have become conditioned to think that God is something other than ourself. We have also been so conditioned by the very nature of the spiritual quest to be always looking and searching, that we tend to turn our attention away from what is present. One friend had a long dream involving intense effort and searching. He was trying to get at a treasure which he had been told was closed up in coffers inside a mausoleum. Despite all his efforts he could not get inside. Then he went back to the beach nearby where the dream had started and began digging for buried treasure. Near to the surface he uncovered some yellow-colored bars, but he could not believe that it was gold because it had been so easy to find.

After a lifetime of searching it can be difficult to learn not to look. This is particularly true in the North American culture where there is a very powerful conditioning that you have to aspire to be other than what you are and that your own life is not good enough. This conditioning drives people remorselessly to work harder and harder to change their life and better their material circumstances. It is a pioneer psychology that has helped to develop America and create a "land of opportunity." But this conditioning has also infected the collective attitude towards spirituality. There is an intense drive to search that overshadows the need to wait for Him, to allow Him to come to us because it is His pleasure. He has buried Himself just beneath the surface of our own hearts, and when we are ready He will show us how close we are to Him.

In being attentive to Him we allow His grace to be infused into our lives. It is His grace that changes our life so that it can embrace Him rather than exclude Him. Our own effort, the effort of "recollection," aligns us with the stream of love that flows between the Creator and the creation. But once we are aligned we need to allow this energy to bring us closer to Him. Surrendering ourselves in contemplation we allow Him to reveal Himself:

> To the one whom God has placed in the rank of His lovers, He gives the vision of Himself, for He has sworn, saying, "By My Glory, I will show him My Face and I will heal his soul by the Vision of Myself."[34]

STAGES OF PRAYER

PART TWO: LIVING IN THE TWO WORLDS

Who in all his work sees God, he in truth goes unto God:
God is his worship, God is his offering,
offered by God in the fire of God.
Bhagavad Gita[1]

ENACTING HIS WILL

The birth of the Self is a state of being in which the psyche of the lover has become the receptive wax for the imprint of the Beloved. We are always waiting, inwardly listening for His hint. Our heart is attuned to the sound of His voice. But in order for this inner relationship to become integrated into consciousness it needs to be lived out in the midst of the world. In alchemical symbolism this stage is called the *rubedo*, the reddening, because in order for an inner process to become alive it must be lived out, it must have "blood," what the alchemists called the "redness" of life. Only when we see the strength and meaning of our inner bond with the Beloved in our outer life do we know that it is real. It is not enough to just listen to His hint, we have to enact it. Then, when we see His mystery unfold around us, every cell of our being recognizes His presence. The inner bond with the Beloved becomes fully alive within the lover. This is always a moment of awe.

The perfect mystic, to quote the Blessed John Ruysbroeck, "dwells in God, and yet he goes out towards created things in the spirit of love towards all things."[2] It is this manifestation of the hidden link of love between the Beloved and His creation that fully transforms the lover. The energy of the Beloved flows from the innermost depths of the psyche out into the world. The whole of the lover, including the physical body, is involved in this process of manifestation, enabling the whole of the lover to be transformed.

Saint Teresa describes this state of uniting the inner and outer life as the third degree of prayer, "union." She writes how it differs from the second degree of prayer, "the prayer of the quiet:"

> In the first state (the prayer of the quiet) the soul does not wish to move or stir but delights in the blessed repose of a Mary, whereas in the second state it can be like Martha also. Thus it is, as it were, leading the active and contemplative life at once, and can apply itself to works of charity, to its professional business and to reading as well. Yet in this state we are not wholly masters of ourselves, but are well aware that the better part of the soul is elsewhere. It is as if we were speaking to one person, while someone else were speaking to us, so that we cannot attend properly to either.[3]

The birth of the Self is an awakening of a higher state of consciousness, as a result of which the best part of the lover's attention remains inwardly focused on the Beloved, inwardly attentive to His will. Saint Teresa remarks that although the soul engages in outer activity, "the better part of the soul is elsewhere." We become aware of our bond with the Beloved, and the more we enact His will in the world the stronger grows our conscious awareness of this inner connection.

However, it does not make everyday life easier, because our inner attention is always somewhere else. As Saint Teresa explains, "It is as if we were speaking to one person, while someone else were speaking to us, so that we cannot attend properly to either." Human relationships are often the first to suffer at this stage, because we cannot fully engage with another human being. The Beloved has taken the best part of us and claimed it for His own. Inwardly we always look towards Him, and our full attention can never be on another. This is one of the great sacrifices made by the lover which results in both joy and pain. Inwardly we know that we always belong, but outwardly we often feel alone, a solitary soldier of the two worlds.

At the beginning this stage of living in the two worlds can be very difficult for the mystic. Mystics are usually introverts, more at home in the inner world than in the outer world. As I have mentioned earlier, they have often been misunderstood since childhood, and even carry the collective shadow of an extrovert society. Furthermore, His lovers often have an instinctual fear of their heart's secret being violated by a world in which they have always felt a stranger. As our meditation and inner work allow us to glimpse the inner dimensions of ourself, we are also aware that these experiences cannot be communicated to the outside world. This is like a curse for the mystic which only grows greater as the inner experiences intensify. The inner reality which becomes a more and more central part of our life isolates us from ordinary people in the sense that only those who have similar experiences can understand us. Sukie Colgrave describes how our relationship with the new-born Self evokes the shadow and the strength of our own aloneness:

To remain loyal to the unfolding Self is to risk rejection and loneliness. For even those closest to us cannot hear directly the voice of our own Self. We are alone with our own dreams, meditations and feelings. Someone conversant with the language of the soul may be able to support us at this time by recognizing and affirming the validity of our perceptions, but the ultimate responsibility and sense of truth is ours alone. It is not comfortable to stand unsupported, cradling one's infant Self in a world which cannot see or hear it and therefore has little respect or understanding for its needs. But the pain and loneliness test and strengthen our capacity to listen to the voice of the soul, rather than the voices of convention and collective morality.[4]

In our aloneness we become more and more focused on the inner relationship with the Self. More and more the Beloved opens us to the mystery of our own being. But we have to accept that the world sees these experiences as meaningless and even dangerous. Going beyond the mind we have entered the reality of love which carries the stamp of madness. Sufis know that the Beloved has a special place in His heart for His own personal idiots, but they also know that they have to live in the world. There is a real truth in the cartoon which depicts the lunatic tied up in a strait-jacket asking the mystic, "How come I'm locked up here and you are walking around free?" To which the mystic replies, "I knew who to say what to and you didn't."

Discrimination is one of the most important qualities which the wayfarer has to learn and we all make mistakes. Often when we have first discovered a spiritual truth we long to share it with others, not realizing that they may be unable to digest it. The following dream showed the dreamer that she lacked this discrimination:

> I am feeding many people. I have a large tub
> of honey and with a spade I take it out and mix
> it with dirt and excrement on the road. It tastes
> disgusting and I wake up feeling sick.

Honey is symbolically a food of the gods and not everyone wants such a food. It cannot be mixed with the dirt and excrement from the road, but rather requires a certain inner purity to be able to be digested. Jung understood this when he wisely said that one should not always tell people the truth: "Truth can be cruel, useless —one must not always tell it, one must tell it when it can be useful, when it can do good."[5]

Not everyone can bear the light of consciousness. Not everyone has the psychological stability to confront the shadow, to come to terms with his own inadequacies and hold together the opposites of his own nature. It is destructive to try and make others "grow up" psychologically unless you *know* that they have the inner foundation to bear the pain that comes with consciousness.

Even more threatening can be words that ring with the silence of the beyond. Spiritual truth can only be hinted at in words that sound paradoxical and are disturbing to the rational mind. Not everyone wants or needs to hear this and uninvited it can even evoke hostility. It is for this reason that one should never invite someone to a Sufi group: a person has to ask. Traditionally the person has to ask three times. Otherwise if you bring someone to a spiritual meeting you are responsible for what it may bring up in them.

But in this dream it is the dreamer who feels sick, because she has polluted her own inner experience by sharing it with those who could not appreciate it. When we have just been given a spiritual insight it is very fragile, our consciousness can only just grasp it. If this inner child is rejected by the cold rational disbelief of others we too can lose touch with it. Our new-born relationship with the beyond can be trampled underfoot by a collective rejection. This is the meaning of Christ's saying:

> Give not that which is holy unto the dogs, neither cast ye your pearls before swine, lest they trample them under their feet, and turn again and rend you.[6]

WORK IN THE WORLD

The Sufi says that one must wait for the right time, the right place and the right people. There does come the time when the outer world is aligned with the inner world in such a way that it is receptive to a new quality of consciousness. As Shakespeare says in *King Lear*, "Ripeness is all,"[7] because what matters in any transition is the state of readiness. The wayfarer learns to watch the signs that indicate it is time to manifest what had been hidden. These signs come from the inner world in the form of dreams and hints; but signs also come from the outer world in a change of situation that can be subtle or dramatic.

In my own personal experience the moment of transition came abruptly one Monday morning. The headmistress of the school in which I was working as an English teacher called me into her office and told me that due to economic reasons the school was contracting and my employment was terminated. I had enjoyed teaching English literature to high-school children, integrating a psychological and spiritual dimension into the academic curriculum. There was also a security in the fact that my spiritual interests were mainly kept separate from my work. Nobody at the school knew about the most important side of my life and so it was protected from ridicule or misunderstandings.

But there comes a point on the path when the inner and outer life cannot be kept separate. The Self, which has been hidden deep in the unconscious, rises into consciousness and needs to express itself in our outer life. The energy of the Self can no longer be contained as a solely inner experience. In this time of birth the Self will attract the outer situation that it needs. In our ego-oriented culture we have forgotten that our outer circumstances are just a reflection of our inner state of being. Furthermore, the Self, "That boundless Power, source of every power,"[8] has the power to change our outer circumstances. This power is most visible in moments of synchronicity, when an inner experience is so powerful that it can manifest itself. For example, a friend dreamt of two black dogs as guardians of the underworld, and then the next day, sitting in the garden of an English country pub, she turned around and saw the same two dogs beside a nearby table!

Just as we learn to listen to the inner world, so we become receptive to the hints from the outer world. In the words of the Qur'an, "And we will show them Our signs in the horizons and in themselves."[9] Sometimes unexpected opportunities present themselves, for, as Joseph Campbell says:

if you follow your bliss you put yourself on a kind of track that has been there all the while, waiting for you, and the life that you ought to be living is the one you are living. When you can see that, you begin to meet people who are in the field of your bliss, and they open the doors to you. I say follow your bliss and don't be afraid and doors will open where you didn't know they were going to be.[10]

But at the beginning there is often the experience that doors are closed behind us. This was my situation. I was out of a job and however hard I tried I could not get another teaching job. Then in a vision I saw a diamond ring on my index finger. A diamond is a symbol of the Self and so I knew that it was time to express what was deepest within me. I wanted to write a thesis on Jungian psychology, which was almost impossible because Jungian psychology is not accepted in the English academic system. But I discovered one person who taught Jungian psychology within the religious department of a university. With the impeccable timing that is often experienced in relationship with the Self, just as I finished my thesis he received his Ph.D. and was able to be my examiner.

The Self embraces both the outer and inner worlds, both body and spirit. But it requires a sacrifice of an ego perspective to our work in order for us to be open to this new dimension. Interestingly there came a point in my thesis when I had to give away all my old English-teaching books before I could progress any further. If I held on to the security of my old identity as an English teacher the new work could not be born.

A transition which includes a sacrifice always has a quality of risk. Following an inner vision means gambling one's outer security. Here again discrimination is of

utmost importance. We need to consider our responsibilities, particularly towards our family. The Sufi places
his family first and has no right to risk their welfare. The
hadîth "First tie your camel's knee and then trust in God"
is invaluable advice. But at the same time the step from
the ego to the Self involves giving up the notion that we
look after ourselves:

> The link which ego consciousness has forged
> between work and material security assumes
> correctly that well-being depends on work; but it
> also assumes that this work has to have a direct
> relationship to money or wealth. While we remain
> bound within the parameters of this ego perspec-
> tive our material survival appears to depend on
> our individual endeavor alone. But as conscious-
> ness shifts from ego to Self, as it relinquishes its
> identification with the personal and ephemeral,
> this perspective changes. . . .For just as the human
> organism is created to feed each cell of the healthy
> individual body, so too does the Self spontane-
> ously feed and take care of each individual being
> no longer isolated from its abundance by limiting
> images, ideas, and feelings of separateness and
> autonomy.[11]

Bhai Sahib expressed the same truth when, talking about
money, he said: "At first the human being relies on
himself, on his own cleverness, but later he is taught to
trust God, and God provides for him. . . ."[12] The Self,
which is not separate from God, provides us with the
material support that we need in order for us to do His
work. However, this *only happens* if the ego is surrendered, thus allowing the Self to manifest in our ordinary
everyday life.

The sacrifice of the ego not only enables us to be looked after, it also leads us into unexpected dimensions of ourself which manifest on a broader horizon than we could have imagined. When I began studying for my Ph.D. I thought that I was just progressing from being a high-school teacher to a career as a university lecturer, teaching a Jungian approach to English literature. Little did I realize that the Self had other plans, and that within four years I would be lecturing all over America on the relationship between Jungian psychology and Sufism.

The Self knows our inner potential and it will prompt and push us to fulfill our deepest destiny. Gradually we learn to trust and to surrender ourselves to its crazy wisdom. If we keep our attention on the inner bond with the Beloved we immerse ourselves in the security of the link of love that unites the inner and outer world. This security of the heart is often very threatening to the mind and the ego, but it allows us to open to the unexpected and enjoy being thrown into the unknown:

> losing through you what seemed myself,i find
> selves unimaginably mine;beyond
> sorrow's own joys and hoping's very fears [13]

However the Self manifests, it means integrating one's inner life with one's outer work rather than keeping the two separate. For one friend this means making jewelry whose symbolism reflects his inner vision. For another it means working as a judge and staying true to her inner principles and feelings of compassion. It always involves a commitment to one's work that reflects the lover's inner commitment to the Beloved.

At the same time this commitment entails the vulnerability of living with an open heart, for it is through the open heart of His lover that the Beloved works in the world. It is easy to open one's heart in the protected space of meditation. But many of us have been wounded by the insensitivity and cruelty of a world that does not understand the ways of the heart. To return to the world with the vulnerability of a lover is a risk that we hesitate to take.

But the world is the place of our voluntary crucifixion which contains the miracle of transformation. As the ego surrenders to the will of the Self, so the lover is embraced by the protective arms of the Beloved in the midst of the world. Suffering is born from ego-attachment, but the commitment of working for the Self together with the fulfillment that comes from this work dissolves the bonds of ego-attachment. When we consciously experience the fulfillment that comes from working for the higher purposes of the Self this so overshadows any fulfillment arising from ego gratification that the ego loses its hold on us. Just as one's inner transformation needs to be lived in the outer world in order to become real, so too do we need to consciously realize the shallowness of ego gratification in order to become free of the ego.

Working from the perspective of the Self also involves the risk of following its guidance which we very often do not understand. In the Qur'an this is exemplified by the story of Khidr, whose behavior appeared criminal to Moses but was rooted in profound meaning.[14] On a daily practical level it often means saying something to a person without fully understanding why. While the world teaches us to think first and say afterwards, Sufis are taught to speak the first thing that comes to our mind, because the first thought comes from God. Though here again discrimination is important because we have to distinguish the voice of the ego from the voice of God in the heart.

At the beginning we often think, "I can't say that." This is particularly true when we are prompted to say something very personal to someone whom we hardly know or may be meeting for the first time. But if we don't say what we should we are usually left with a feeling of something being painfully unfulfilled—we have let down the Self. When we do speak what our heart prompts we are often amazed by the response, as the words open a locked door in the listener or touch upon something that is crying out to be discussed. The more we learn to blindly follow our inner guidance the easier it becomes, because we see how it works. We see how the hand of the Beloved touches those around us.

One of the fears that can hold us back from enacting the will of the Self is that of making mistakes, saying or doing things that are embarrassing or wrong. Of course we will make mistakes. But there is a spiritual law that we are always given an opportunity to correct a mistake— His mercy is always greater than His justice. We work for the will of the Beloved and are prepared to learn from any mistake that we may make. It is only the arrogance of the ego that is afraid of being wrong. My teacher said that she didn't mind anymore if she made a mistake because she was happy to apologize in humility. She had already lost everything and there was nothing left to lose. To fully accept that we are human is to accept that we will make mistakes, and the more we become immersed in the Self the less we care what others may think. We relate directly to the Beloved and not to the world's opinion.

A FEATHER ON THE BREATH OF GOD

So far I have discussed this stage of transition from the perspective of the ego, looking at the loneliness, vulnerability and sense of risk that can be evoked by integrating the two worlds. But the soul experiences this transition as an unfolding that enables its depth of meaning and beauty to be expressed in the outer world. In the following dream the symbolic imagery of the soul describes how this transition appears from an inner perspective:

> I am in a space in the universe of total darkness. I have a light at my right side. Through the darkness a beautiful big blue feather comes towards me. As it comes closer I can see that it is being carried by a black butterfly with four symmetrical wings. The butterfly seems to be making a great effort to bring it to me. Then there is a desk and the feather has a porcelain tip which will allow me to use it as a pen.

The dream begins in the darkness, in the unknown. This darkness is the home of the mystic. It is the divine darkness, the cloud of unknowing, "the black light of the *Deus absconditus*, the hidden treasure that aspires to reveal itself."[15] It is the nothingness of God that exists before the creation and that exists after the creation. The astronauts experienced this total darkness on the physical level as the spaces between the stars. They were overwhelmed by its intensity. "It was a texture," Charles Duke commented. "I felt like I could reach out and touch it. It was so intense. The blackness was so intense." Eugene Cernan described the Earth as "moving in a blackness that is almost beyond conception." He continues:

> The Earth is surrounded by blackness though you're looking through sunlight. There is only light if the sunlight has something to shine on.

When the sun shines through space it's black. All
because the light doesn't strike anything. The light
doesn't strike anything so all you see is black.[16]

Cernan is describing a physical truth that is also a
fundamental mystical experience. In deep states of
meditation there is absolute stillness, darkness and
nothingness because there is nobody there to reflect the
light. To quote Irina Tweedie: "We leave the mind
completely behind us in order to enter the uncreated,
dark light of God."[17]

In the state of *fanâ* the lover is lost in the nothingness of Truth, in the empty fullness of the Self. But in this
dream the dreamer is not yet totally absorbed into
nothingness for there is still the duality of her and the
space. At her right side is the light of consciousness. She
is not yet fully merged into the dazzling darkness. The
dream points her towards union with the outer world so
that she can lose herself more completely in the Beloved.

Through the darkness there comes towards the
dreamer "a beautiful big blue feather." Birds belong to
the element of air and symbolize our aspirations. A
feather is a symbol of spiritual truth. In *The Conference
of the Birds* the first manifestation of the Simurgh, the
mythological bird that symbolizes the Self, was one of his
feathers that fell on China. The Christian mystic, Hildegard
von Bingen, who lived both the inner and outer life to the
full (she was an abbess, visionary, healer, painter,
musician, scientist, as well as being involved in politics
and diplomacy), used the image of a feather to describe
herself:

Listen: there was once a king sitting on his
throne. Around him stood great and wonderfully
beautiful columns ornamented with ivory, bear-

ing the banners of the king with great honor. Then
it pleased the king to raise a small feather from the
ground and he commanded it to fly. The feather
flew, not because of anything in itself but because
the air blew it along. Thus am I a feather on the
breath of God.[18]

The dreamer's feather is blue, symbolizing her own
feminine self and the devotion which is a quality of the
lover. Devotion is an attitude of surrender in which one's
whole self is in service to the Beloved. It is only through
an attitude of devotion that one's inner being is able to
act in the outer world without being polluted by the
desires of the ego. Devotion also unites the two worlds,
for through the lover's devotion to the Beloved the inner
and outer worlds are able to merge in a state of oneness
in which everything is embraced by His presence. It is
through the lover that the Beloved is able to embrace His
creation. The attitude of devotion creates a space in
which this can happen.

As the feather nears the dreamer she sees for the first
time that it is being carried by "a black butterfly with four
symmetrical black wings." A butterfly is a symbol of the
soul and of transformation. In Saint Teresa's account of
the soul's progress, *Interior Castle*, she likens the seeker
to a silkworm. Through our meditations, prayers and
devotional work we spin a cocoon in which we then die
and are reborn as a white butterfly.[19.] Through the
dreamer's inner efforts she has given birth to herself as
a butterfly, whose four symmetrical wings represent the
quaternio, a symbol of wholeness and the Self.

The dreamer's butterfly is black. Black is the color of
the nothingness. It is the garment of the mystic symbolizing spiritual poverty and renunciation. True renunciation is a state of detachment in which the lover realizes

that he can only be fulfilled by the Beloved: "The reality of poverty is that one becomes rich through God alone; its outer guise is non-attention to ways and means."[20] In this sense it is a state of total surrender to the will of the Beloved. Not only the ego but the whole being of the lover is given to God for Him to do with as He will.

In this dream it is the butterfly, the soul, that wears the black color of poverty. The real surrender happens on the level of the soul. This is the state of holy abandonment symbolized by the Virgin Mary, whom the Sufis regard as the typification of the mystic soul that enables the spiritual Child to be conceived and then born.[21] It is through this innermost surrender that the essence of the lover is united with the Beloved, thus allowing the Beloved to live through the lover, to be "the eye by which he sees and the ear by which he hears."[22] On the Sufi path the soul of the lover is united with the soul of the teacher, whose soul is united with God. Thus poverty is associated with *fanâ*, the process in which the wayfarer is first annihilated in the teacher and then in God.

Only when the soul is surrendered, merged into the emptiness, is His stamp impressed upon the heart. Naqshband means, in Persian, "The Impressor" or "The Engraver," because, as I have discussed in detail elsewhere,[23] this process of mystical impression is central to the Naqshbandi system. But Saint Teresa uses the same image of an impression to describe "what God does to the soul so that it may know itself to be His:"

> That soul has so delivered itself into His hands and His great love has so completely subdued it that it neither knows nor desires anything save that God will do with it what He wills. Never, I think, will God grant this favor save to the soul which He takes for His very own. His will is that,

without understanding how, the soul shall go thence sealed with His seal. In reality, the soul in that state does no more than the wax when a seal is impressed upon it—the wax does not impress itself; it is only prepared for the impress: that is, it is soft—and it does not even soften itself so as to be prepared; it merely remains quiet and consenting. Oh, goodness of God, that all this shall be done at Thy cost! Thou does require only our wills and does ask that Thy wax may offer no impediment.[24]

The surrender of the soul is the essential poverty of the heart, and it is within the heart that the lover experiences the total blackness and emptiness that is the true face of the Beloved. When the eleventh-century Sufi, Abu'l-Hasan Kharaqânî, was asked for the sign of poverty, he replied, "that the heart be black." "Meaning what?" he was questioned. He replied, "No other color exists beyond black."[25] This blackness is the hidden treasure that the lover carries as a stamp in the innermost recesses of the heart. It is the pre-existing memory of the state of union before separation.

His lovers are those who drank the wine of love at the day of the primordial covenant and surrendered their souls to the Beloved before the creation. They belong to the Beloved from pre-eternity—He has already taken them for His very own. Their work is to bring this state of surrender into consciousness and live it in the world. In this dream the black butterfly comes out of the total darkness pushing a feather which becomes a pen. The lover thus becomes an unknowing instrument in the hands of the Beloved; in the words of Mother Teresa of Calcutta: "I don't claim anything of the work. I am a little pencil in His hand. That is all. He does the thinking. He does the writing. The pencil has nothing to do with it."[26]

The birth of the Self is the birth into consciousness of the lover's inner attitude of surrender and devotion. Thus the lover remains in a state of detachment that enables him to work in the world without being seduced by its myriad attractions. I once had a dream in which I was in a three-storey shopping center. It had many restaurants offering different types of food. I walked through the shopping center from the first to the third floor, but none of these restaurants interested me. Then I went up to the fourth floor on the roof where I was given a pen with a gold arrow. To be a pen in the hands of the Beloved is to manifest surrender into service. Sufis are known as "slaves of the One and servants of the many" because they are surrendered to the Beloved and are thus able to serve His creation.

THE REAL ATTENTION

First the wayfarer turns his attention away from the world and slowly breaks the bonds of ego-attachment that imprison him. The ego surrenders to the will of the Self and thus creates a space for the inborn state of the surrender of the soul to be made manifest. This state of surrender is the bond between the lover and the Beloved. It manifests as a detachment from the outer world that is born from a sense of belonging to Him rather than from rejecting the world. It is in this sense that the lover does not renounce anything; rather the attachments of the world fall away. In my dream of the shopping center I did not reject the food offered by the restaurants, it just did not interest me. My attention had been turned elsewhere.

Inwardly the Self always looks towards God. This is the "real attention" but this real attention "is by nature suppressed. Only the Realized Soul can awaken it, i.e., the Guru."[27] Then the mind is turned in the opposite direction, away from the world, towards God. When the lover's attention is securely focused on the Beloved he can work in the world without being distracted. Life then carries the hidden joy of the heart, as Irina Tweedie describes:

> Life is never so real or beautiful. The difference is, however, that we are no longer chasing after it and its pleasures. We have the taste of something infinitely more precious. My life is at an end, but I tell you that flowers have never looked so red; nor has food tasted so good as it does now. And yet I am not chasing after these things, the things of the world. There is something I cannot name which is lovelier still. It is nowhere else; it is here, but it is not of this world.[28]

At the beginning the wayfarer needs to make every effort to turn his attention away from the world. But as the real attention of the soul is awakened and born into consciousness then this inner bond of the heart dissolves our outer attachments. Effortlessly we are embraced by the larger dimension of the Self. Then our work is to stay surrendered so that the Beloved can be experienced in our daily life as something both intimate and endless, as e.e.cummings joyously exclaims:

> i carry your heart with me(i carry it in
> my heart)i am never without it(anywhere
> i go you go, my dear;and whatever is done
> by only me is your doing, my darling)

                                              i fear
no fate(for you are my fate,my sweet)i want
no world(for beautiful you are my world, my true)
and it's you are whatever a moon has always meant
and whatever a sun will always sing is you

here is the deepest secret nobody knows
(here is the root of the root and the bud of the bud
and the sky of the sky of a tree called life;which grows
higher than soul can hope or mind can hide)
and this is the wonder that's keeping the stars apart

i carry your heart(i carry it in my heart) [29]

HOLDING HIS LIGHT IN THE WORLD

The lover's inner attention dwells with the Beloved and
his outer attention is in the world; thus the lover unites
these apparent opposites. Through the heart of His lover
the Beloved can then enter and influence His creation. It
is in this sense that His lovers are points of light; places
where He can unfold the hidden purpose of His creation.
The deepest joy of the mystic is that he can participate in
this work.

The Sufi sees the purpose of creation expressed in
the *hadîth qudsî*: "I was a hidden treasure and I wanted
to be known, so I created the world." The Beloved
awakens the lover so that He can use the lover's eyes to
see Himself—"I created perception in thee only that
therein I might become the object of My perception."[30]
Through the eyes of the lover the Beloved can see
Himself reflected in His creation. If the lover stands in the

midst of the world the Beloved can see His beauty and His majesty where it is most hidden: in the marketplace. He can see His face in the midst of the bustle and clamour of the world. What this means is that the world of matter is then embraced by the Beloved's knowledge of Himself. As He becomes conscious of Himself in the midst of the world, so the light of His consciousness illumines the midst of the world, enabling people to see Him in their ordinary, daily life as never before, for only "In thy light shall we see light."

As the Beloved becomes conscious of Himself in the midst of the world, so can those who live in the midst of the world become conscious of Him. We are part of Him and so we participate in His knowledge of Himself. Those who are closest to Him know this more fully than those whose hearts are less open to Him. For many people this secret is hidden too deep for them to find it. But they are still included and will feel the quality of life begin to change. A sense of belonging will begin to permeate a world dominated by the feelings of separation and isolation. A depth of meaning will surface amidst the most mundane activities.

The work of His lovers is to hold the consciousness of this change; to recognize that the real meaning of transformation is the Beloved coming closer to Himself within the hearts of people and within the collective heart of the world. This consciousness is held in the web of light that is being woven around the world. If we do not hold this consciousness then the present time of global transition will not have any lasting effect. The same ego patterns will dominate the coming age and there will have been no evolution of consciousness.

When an individual goes through a powerful inner experience or time of transition it is very important that the meaning of the experience is made conscious.

Otherwise, to quote T.S. Eliot, "We had the experience but missed the meaning."[31] We need to make conscious the meaning of the present time of global transformation and then to hold that meaning so that it does not fall back into the unconscious. At the primordial covenant, when the not-yet-created humanity responded to God's question, "Am I not your Lord?" with the word *balâ*, "Yes, we witness it," His lovers wrote their names in the notebooks of love, vowing to uphold this real purpose of consciousness: that creation recognizes the Creator. For centuries they have kept their pledge as a secret, as a solitary recognition within the heart. But as the web of light is being woven around the world, so this inner consciousness of His lovers is being bonded together to form the foundation of a new collective consciousness. It is this collective consciousness that will hold the innermost meaning of the present time of global transition and so help a lasting transformation to take place.

But His lovers always remember that this transformation can only take place if it is His will. This attitude of surrender is an essential part of their work because it recognizes that He will only become known to the world if He wills it. The surrendering of the individual will to His will helps His consciousness to enter a world which has become dominated by the ego, by individual consciousness. It is only His consciousness, which the individual experiences as the higher consciousness of the Self, that can transform our world.

STAGES OF PRAYER

PART THREE: ECSTASY

That we may merge into the deep and dazzling darkness,
vanish into it, dissolve in it forever in an unbelievable
bliss beyond imagination, for absolute nothingness
represents absolute bliss.

Gregory of Nyssa

THE SONG OF THE SOUL

The Sufi is trained to live in the world of spirit and the world of matter and bond the two together within his heart. The flow of love that permeates creation is the substance of this bond. Love sustains the world of matter and the unfolding pattern of creation because it embodies the relationship of the Creator with His creation. Every atom unconsciously sings of its love for the Creator, reflecting back to Him both His majesty and His beauty:

> The world is charged with the grandeur of God.
> It will flame out, like shining from shook foil. . . [1]

But His lovers are those whom He has chosen to make this hidden secret *conscious*, to *consciously* recognize the link of love that sustains the world.

When the bond of love between the Creator and His creation is made conscious then the song of the world soul can be heard beneath the noise of the marketplace. As individual lovers link themselves together then this song begins to surface within the collective consciousness of mankind. This song holds the purpose of our planet's evolution and embraces the destiny of every human being. Moreover, as much as it is the song of the world soul, so is it the song of every individual soul. The world's song is not other than our own song because we are an integral part of the whole. We are a part of the great oneness, as the mystic knows from his own experience.

The song of the world soul is our own song, and yet as we are each unique individuals so is our own song unique. It is written in the Qur'an that "Every being has his own appropriate mode of prayer and glorification."[2] On the level of the ego the collective denies the individual, and many people repress their individuality in order to fit into a collective social group. But on the level of the soul the collective enhances individuality: our own individual life becomes more meaningful when it is experienced in relationship to the larger pattern of life.

The way the collective enhances individuality can be explained on a psychological level. To a much greater degree than is commonly appreciated we are in the hands of the gods, influenced by the primordial forces that were once depicted in ancient mythologies and are now mainly experienced in dreams. To become conscious of these forces would suggest a loss of individuality, yet, paradoxically, the reverse is true. It was the gods who gave direction to men's lives. It is the archetypes that give meaning to our individual lives. Jung defines individuality as "that which is unique in the combination of collective elements of the persona and its manifestations."[3] Our individuality gains a deeper significance when we appreciate the collective elements that so influence us. It is for this reason that many people are interested in astrology. In astrology the collective elements are seen as the planets and houses of the horoscope that combine to make an individual chart. A personal situation can appear more meaningful when we appreciate the collective forces, or "stars," that appear to influence us. As our individual existence takes on an archetypal perspective, so we cease to be the playthings of the gods, and become an integral and meaningful part of their cosmic drama.

Through a relationship with the archetypes we are able to appreciate the depth and significance of our own individuality. When we hear our own song as a part of the world song it has a richness, passion and purpose born from the integration of the individual with the whole. It is only in relation to the whole that we can appreciate the full range of our own potential, for the simple reason that our life has a purpose beyond our individual self. When we hear the song of the world soul our own song resonates with this deeper destiny.

At the present time our collective consciousness is being attuned to the world's song, enabling it to be heard more clearly than ever before. His lovers are helping in this work through holding His consciousness in their hearts. They hold this link of love that is the primal note in the song of every soul. It is through this link that we are able to realize the essence of our own existence, and through this same link He can become manifest in His own world. In the words of Ibn 'Arabî:

> God is necessary to us in order that we may exist, while we are necessary to Him in order that He may be manifested to Himself—I give Him also life, by knowing Him in my heart.[4]

When this primal note of the heart is heard in the song of the world soul the Beloved can be born within our collective consciousness. What this might mean we can only begin to imagine because it points to a collective consciousness infused with the energy of the Self.

It is the energy of the Self that transforms individual consciousness. The Self is both individual and universal: "the individual self . . . is the universal Self, maker of past and future."[5] Our individual essence is identical with the infinite, omnipotent power that is the root of everything. Yet although this energy is all-pervading it is also separate from ego-consciousness. If the collective consciousness of humanity is infused with this divine energy and able to contain it then there is a possibility for a global transformation that reflects the wholeness of the Self. Our need for a unified global awareness which embraces all aspects of life on this planet would not be just a utopian vision but a psychological possibility.

At the present time we are faced with the fragmentation of old power structures dissolving and an ecological crisis brought about by ego-oriented greed. If the energy of the Self is held in the consciousness of mankind then this dangerous time of transition can connect us with a higher destiny before new ego-patterns are created. There is space for the Self to manifest and realign mankind with the real purpose of consciousness.

In the past era we have used the divine gift of consciousness to develop the ego. In the West we have asserted ourselves at the cost of the earth, putting our personal well-being above any global consideration. Circumstances have now evoked a need for a collective consciousness that goes beyond the ego. Ecological global responsibility points to our need to *consciously* accept the guardianship of the planet with which we were entrusted so long ago. This is our collective destiny which cannot be appreciated from the isolated perspective of the ego. It belongs to the larger horizons of the Self, and yet it is impressing itself upon our daily life as we are made increasingly aware that we are destroying the very ecosystems that sustain us.

Jung said that we never *solve* major problems but we *grow out* of them. It is only too obvious that our present global problems cannot be solved unless we collectively grow out of our ego-oriented approach. The energy of the Self presents us with the possibility for transformation, but it requires our conscious co-operation. His lovers know that the essence of this work is surrender. Human beings have free will and the energy of the Self cannot manifest without the voluntary surrender of the ego. Each in our own way we need to look beyond the desires of the ego to the need of the soul. Only when we live from our own inner core are we in harmony with the whole. Plotinus says:

> We are like a choir who stand round the conductor, but we do not always sing in tune, because our attention is diverted by looking at external things. So we always move around the One—if we did not we would dissolve and cease to exist—but we do not always look towards the One. Hence, instead of that free and conscious co-operation in the great life of All which alone can make personal life worth living, we move like slaves or marionettes, and oblivious to the whole to which our little steps contribute, fail to observe the measure whereto the worlds keep time.

But when we look inwards towards the center, towards Him who is our conductor, "Then we no longer sing out of tune, but form a truly divine chorus about Him."[6]

NEED AND WANT

In the Sufi tale, *The Story of Moshkel Gosha*, there is a poor woodcutter whose daughter becomes unsatisfied with her ordinary daily food. She asks her father for something different to eat. She symbolizes his anima, his soul figure which asks for something other than ordinary ego consciousness.

At first the woodcutter works harder and chops more wood, hoping to earn enough to buy the food she wants. The woodcutter tries to answer the needs of the soul from the perspective of the ego and the old patterns of conditioning. In the same way people often try to fulfill an inner dissatisfaction by working harder, buying a new car or taking a holiday. But, as with the woodcutter, this does not work. Everything goes wrong for the woodcutter and he is left tired and desperate. Then he hears a voice which tells him, "If you *need* enough and *want* little enough you shall find delicious food." Our inner need, the need of the soul, is only answered if it is great enough, for then the human being calls out in such a way that the call must be answered: answered, however it may appear, by the Higher Self. This is the value of despair, for when we reach a point of total despair we call out in great need and that call is always answered. But here lies the significance of the second condition, to "*want* little enough." For while the answer is always there, if the demands of the ego are too loud we cannot hear it.

Our present global situation combines a growing ecological disaster with an increasing inner hunger. We *need* enough. The woodcutter, having reached the point of desperation, is given precious stones, symbolizing the energy of the Self. Although it is not yet known to many people, even those looking seriously at the problem, our

107

global need has evoked a similar response: our collective psyche is being infused with the energy of the Self. This energy, this "boundless power, source of every power," can both heal the planet and provide us with the nourishment we crave.

However, in the West our inner hunger has combined with our greed to bombard us with desires. We have so long neglected the needs of the soul that we confuse its hunger with the ego's desires, and try to satisfy the soul with material possessions, or the addictive attractions of drugs, alcohol and sex. Now our real test is to learn to "*want* little enough"—to surrender our desires so that we can be responsive to the needs of the soul, hear its song amidst the clamour of the world. When our consciousness is attuned to this song, which is both our individual song and also the song of the world's soul, then the energy of the Self can manifest in our daily lives. This process is already beginning, but it needs our conscious co-operation. We need to surrender so that "Thy will be done on earth as it is in heaven."

EMBRACING UNKNOWINGNESS

But the real focus of the wayfarer always remains inward. Meister Eckhart says "the best and noblest way in which thou mayst come into this Life is by keeping silence and letting God work and speak."[7] In the state of union the lover experiences a deep inner silence and stillness that cannot be disturbed by his outer life. All the people whom he contacts in his daily life, however noisy or disturbing, no longer affect his inner peace. Whatever his outward activity he remains inwardly free. His real attention is always directed towards the inner silence that is the meeting place with the Beloved.

This silence does not belong to the ordinary consciousness of the mind. It is the nothingness of the beyond. Slowly we become familiar with this constant inner emptiness that underlies our consciousness. It is in this space that we remain inwardly attentive to the Beloved, always receptive to His hint. However, as Saint Teresa said, it is at times difficult to function on the inner and outer planes simultaneously—"as if we were speaking to one person, while someone else were speaking to us."

Gradually the mind becomes familiar with the way the Beloved speaks to the lover and learns not to interfere. The foundation of stillness enables the mind to function with a new-found clarity, and it learns to distinguish the voice of the ego from the voice of the Self. When the higher knowledge of the Self comes into consciousness the mind learns not to identify with it. Suddenly one knows something. It could be easy for the ego to become inflated, but it is usually so apparent that this knowledge comes from the beyond that the mind can recognize its origin. This knowledge has a quality that is different from ordinary knowledge—there is not a process of understanding something; suddenly the knowledge is there.

Sometimes, though, this knowledge comes like a seed which the mind has to elaborate in order to convey its full meaning. The mind has to integrate a higher level of perception into ordinary consciousness.

As the mind becomes familiar with this higher knowledge so it learns to trust it without understanding. Unlike Moses we do not continually question the wisdom of Khidr, the Sufi figure who symbolizes direct revelation. In the story in the Qur'an, Khidr tells Moses, "You will not be able to bear with me. For how can you bear with that which is beyond your knowledge?" Although Moses says that he will not question him, he cannot unconditionally accept Khidr's actions, as, for example, when Khidr bores a hole in the boat of a poor fisherman. Three times Moses questions Khidr and then he has to separate from him. Unlike Moses, the lover learns to follow Khidr unquestioningly.

The higher wisdom enters ordinary consciousness through the mind's being immersed in emptiness. Sometimes the lover is conscious of this process. The mind just suddenly goes. At the beginning it can be very disturbing to find your mind disappearing. You can be having a conversation with a friend and what you are about to say goes from your mind. Your attention has been called somewhere else and the mind surrenders and is lost in the higher mind which it cannot grasp. At these times you cannot fully function on both planes, and you just wait for the mind to come back.

In meditation the mind goes completely and it can be lost for hours. In waking consciousness, when the mind is immersed in nothingness, enough of the mind remains to allow one to function on the physical plane, but one cannot think very coherently. The mind usually goes for short periods of time, a few seconds or possibly minutes. However, during these experiences, one is infinitely protected. One is with the Beloved and held in His hands.

A friend was crossing a busy street outside a main railway terminal in London. Suddenly she found that a taxi driver was hooting his car horn at her. As she looked at him she saw that he was incredibly beautiful. Somebody saw that she was standing dazed in the middle of the traffic and came and helped her across the road. She also found this person radiantly beautiful. In the middle of the road she had had a real mystical experience which revealed the radiant beauty that is in all things. She had gone somewhere else but no harm had come to her. Throughout that day at work she was unable to function very well but nobody minded. The dynamic energy of the Self affects our surroundings and causes people to respond in unexpected ways. Another friend had a powerful mystical experience while teaching a class of adolescent schoolchildren. He was unable to teach the rest of the lesson, but the usually lively children just sat quietly in a meditative state!

Such experiences are rare, but they testify to the power of the inner world. Usually the mind goes for a short while and the wayfarer becomes accustomed to the limitations of having his attention turned elsewhere. He learns to adapt his outer circumstances to these limitations. For example, at times it is best not to try and drive a car, but to let someone else drive or not to travel until the experience has passed.

No longer disturbed by states of mindlessness, the lover surrenders to the experience, gladly accepting that he is functioning on a different plane of consciousness. Sometimes the mind returns imprinted with a certain knowledge that is needed at that moment. But often the mind returns empty. There are many different levels of consciousness and a mind whose purpose is to function in the physical world cannot grasp what happens on the inner planes. Bhai Sahib told Irina Tweedie, "What can be understood by the mind is not a high state."

The continual practice of meditation also helps the wayfarer to become accustomed to states of mindlessness. At the same time it tunes him into the higher frequencies of the inner planes. In meditation the individual mind is thrown into the universal mind. This is first experienced in the state of *dhyana* which is:

> . . . the first stage after transcending the think-
> ing faculty of the mind, and from the point of view
> of the intellect it must be considered as an uncon-
> scious state. It is the first step beyond conscious-
> ness as we know it, which will lead eventually, by
> easy degrees, into the state *samadhi*, the super-
> conscious state. The highest stages of *dhyana* are
> gradually transformed into the lower stage of
> *samadhi*, which is still not completely
> conscious. The higher state of *samadhi* represents
> a full awakening of one's own divinity.[8]

The state of *dhyana* is the complete abstraction of the
senses, and since the most similar previous experience to
that is sleep, the mind may mistakenly interpret *dhyana*
at first as sleep. In fact it is a highly dynamic state in which
the lover is immersed in the infinite nothingness of the
Beloved.

AWAKENING IN NOTHINGNESS

Gradually the wayfarer awakens in a state of consciousness in which the ordinary mind is not present. At first
these states may be disturbing and even cut off through
fear. But later they are welcomed and bring a profound
sense of inner security. Real belonging can never be
understood on the level of the mind because this
belonging happens only on the level of the Self. But in
order to reach this state we have to go through the
insecurities of the mind and our fear of the unknowable.

As the inner connection with the Self becomes
stronger, so the disciple is able to live at the higher
vibration of the Self. The ordinary mind cannot retain

these higher frequencies, in the same way that the human ear cannot hear higher frequencies of sound. Thus more and more of the wayfarer's experiences cannot be grasped by the ordinary mind, which is often left in a state of confusion. In *The Conference of the Birds* 'Attâr describes this stage as the Valley of Astonishment and Bewilderment, and he illustrates it with the story of the princess who falls in love with a slave. After drinking a goblet of drugged wine the slave is taken to her chamber, where he spends the night in bliss with her. He is then given another drink of drugged wine and awakes in his own quarters. He is unable to understand what has happened:

> I am in a tumult because what I have seen has happened to me in another body. While hearing nothing I have heard everything, while seeing nothing I have seen everything. . . . What can be more puzzling than something which is neither revealed nor hidden? What I have seen I can never forget, yet I have no idea where it happened. For one whole night I revelled with a beauty who is without equal. Who or what she is I do not know. Only love remains, and that is all. But God knows the truth.[9]

In the states of *dhyana* the lover is immersed in unconsciousness. But gradually a higher level of consciousness begins to awaken. This higher consciousness functions in a different way from the ordinary mind. It does not function through the separation of subject and object, but through immersion in oneness. This can be experienced to a lesser degree in ordinary life; for example, if we concentrate on something we become the object of our concentration for a while. When we learn something we immerse ourself in a subject, and we lose the sense of separation between ourself and the subject. In this experience we also often lose the sense of time. This is a reflection of the real experience of union of subject and object, which happens on a higher level of consciousness, beyond time. Plotinus describes the real mystical experience of union:

> Then the soul neither sees, nor distinguishes
> by seeing, nor imagines that there are two things;
> but becomes as it were another thing, ceases to be
> itself and belong to itself. It belongs to God and
> is one with Him, like two concentric circles:
> concurring they are One; but when they separate
> they are two. . . . Since in this conjunction with the
> Deity there were not two things, but the perceiver
> was one with the perceived.[10]

The more the lover is immersed in the Beloved the greater become the experiences of oneness. These states cannot be described or understood by the ordinary mind. Only, it can be helpful for the mind to understand that it is unable to understand. Then it will surrender more gladly into these states of unknowingness. As Saint Teresa explains, "we understand by not understanding:"

> The will must be fully occupied in loving, but
> it does not understand how it loves. If it under-
> stands it does not understand how it understands,
> or at least, cannot comprehend anything of what
> it understands. I do not think that it understands
> at all, because, as I have said, it does not under-
> stand itself. Nor can I myself understand this.[11]

Union is a state of absolute stillness, darkness and nothingness. It is a oneness with something that is nothing. Saint Teresa, trying to describe this fourth state of prayer, writes that the soul is utterly dissolved in God. Without subject or object there is "enjoyment without any knowledge of what is being enjoyed."[12] In this sense there is no separate identity and thus there is no one there to make any effort. In her image of watering the garden there is no longer a gardener, only the Lord Himself, and "the rain comes down abundantly to soak and saturate the garden."

Through meditation the lover inwardly opens to the silence of the soul where the Beloved is always present. Here the lover and Beloved meet, and the lover surrenders into the emptiness. In the formlessness of love he is absorbed deeper and deeper until he is so lost that there is only the ecstasy of unknowing. The anonymous author of *The Cloud of Unknowing* describes this as the "highest part of contemplation" which "hangeth all wholly in this darkness and in this cloud of unknowing; with a loving striving and a blind beholding unto the naked being of God Himself only."[13]

THE DHIKR

*A breath that does not repeat the name of God
is a wasted breath.*

Kabir

THE SILENT DHIKR

Naqshbandi Sufis are known as the silent Sufis. They practice the silent meditation of the heart and the silent *dhikr*, in distinction to other Sufi orders which practice the vocal *dhikr*. Bahâ'ad-dîn Naqshband said, "God is silence and is most easily reached in silence," and Bhai Sahib elaborates on this: "We are free. We go to the Absolute Truth in silence, for it can be found only in silence and it is silence. That's why we are called the Silent Yogis. If some practices are given, they are performed always in silence."[1]

The practice of the silent *dhikr* became established by 'Abd al-Khâliq Ghujduwânî (d. 1220-21), a disciple of Yûsuf Hamadânî (d. 1140). Yusuf Hamadânî was the first of the *khwâjagân*, or masters of wisdom, who gave the identity to the Sufi Order that then took its name from Bahâ'ad-dîn Naqshband. According to tradition, while 'Abd al-Khâliq Ghujduwânî was studying in Bukhara, he came across the Qur'anic verse (7:55), "call upon your Lord in supplication and hiddenness." He was unable to discover its interpretation until Khidr appeared "to instruct him in the method of the silent *dhikr*. Khidr caused him to repeat the divine name three times while submerged in water, a circumstance of both practical and symbolic significance."² 'Abd al-Khâliq Ghujduwânî was known as the master of the masters, and although he lived a century before Bahâ' ad-dîn Naqshband, Bahâ' ad-dîn "received his mystical upbringing from the 'spiritual presence' of 'Abd al-Khâliq Ghujduwânî." 'Abd al-Khâliq Ghujduwânî taught him "to practice the silent *dhikr* and to abstain from the publicly performed or vocal *dhikr.*"³

The *dhikr* is the repetition of a sacred word or phrase. It can be the *shahâda*, "*Lâ ilâha illâ 'llâh,*" but it is often one of the names or attributes of God.⁴ It is said that God has ninety-nine names, but foremost among these is Allâh. Allâh is His greatest name and contains all His divine attributes.

When Abû Sa'îd ibn Abî'l-Khayr heard the verse from the Qur'an, "Say Allâh! then leave them to amuse themselves in their folly,"⁵ his heart was opened. He gave up his scholarly studies and retired to the niche of the chapel in his house, where for seven years he repeated "Allâh! Allâh! Allâh!" . . . "until at last every atom of me began to cry aloud, 'Allâh! Allâh! Allâh!'" He tells the story that first alerted him to the importance of this *dhikr*. He was with Shaykh Abû 'l-Fadl Hasan, and when the Shaykh picked up a book and began to peruse it, Abû Sa'îd, being a scholar, couldn't help wondering what the book was. The Shaykh perceived his thought and said:

> Abû Sa'îd! All the hundred-and-twenty-four-thousand prophets were sent to preach one word. They bade the people say "Allâh!" and devote themselves to Him. Those who heard this word with the ear alone, let it go out by the other ear; but those who heard it with their souls imprinted it on their souls and repeated it until it penetrated their hearts and souls, and their whole

being became this word. They were made inde-
pendent of the pronunciation of the word, they
were released from the sound and the
letters. Having understood the spiritual meaning
of this word, they became so absorbed in it that
they were no more conscious of their own non-
existence.[6]

According to an esoteric Sufi tradition, the word
Allâh is composed of the article *al*, and *lâh*, one of the
interpretations of which is "nothing." Thus the actual
word Allâh means "the Nothing." For the Sufi the fact that
His greatest name means "the Nothing" has great significance, because Truth, or God, is experienced as the
Nothingness. And one of the mysteries of the path is that
this Emptiness, this Nothingness, loves you. It loves you
with such intimacy and tenderness and infinite
understanding. It loves you from the very inside of your
heart, from the core of your own being. It is not separate
from you. Sufis are lovers and the Nothingness is the
Greatest Beloved in whose embrace the lover completely
disappears.

Shortly before his death, Bhai Sahib said,"There is
nothing but Nothingness." He repeated it twice and Irina
Tweedie understood it as his special message to her. It
points to the very essence of the Sufi path, as Irina
Tweedie explains:

There is nothing but Nothingness. . . . Nothingness in the triune, triple sense: Nothingness because
the little self (the ego) has to go. One has to become nothing. Nothingness, because the higher
states of consciousness represent nothingness to
the mind, for it cannot reach there. It is completely
beyond the range of perception. Complete com-

prehension on the level of the mind is not possible, so one is faced with nothingness. And in the last, most sublime, sense, it is to merge into the Luminous Ocean of the Infinite. I think this is how one has to understand it; that is how Bhai Sahib had meant it, when he spoke of the Nothingness and of the One.[7]

Thus, the name Allâh contains the essence of all Sufi teaching: to become nothing, to become annihilated in Him, so that all that remains is His Infinite Emptiness. This is the path of love, it is the cup of wine which is drunk by His lovers. In the words of Rûmî:

> I drained this cup:
> there is nothing, now,
> but ecstatic annihilation.[8]

REMEMBRANCE

At the core of the *dhikr* is the principle of remembrance, for the Sufi seeks to remember the Beloved in every thought, with each and every breath. Through continually repeating His name we remember Him, not just in the mind but in the heart, and finally there comes the time when every cell of the body endlessly repeats the *dhikr*, endlessly repeats His name.

At first we have to consciously remember to say the *dhikr*. Often the outside world or our own mind distracts us and we forget. When we again remember we may blame ourself for forgetting. But this is just the ego saying, "I should have done better." Rather than blaming oneself it is better to thank Him for reminding us. Then we turn our attention away from the ego towards the Beloved.

Whenever we can we repeat His name, while we are walking or driving. If we say the *dhikr* while we cook then the food is infused with His name. Awake at night we say the name of our Beloved and no moment is wasted. Whenever we can we remember Him. When we are talking or reading we cannot consciously say the *dhikr*, but as the months go by a magic happens: His name starts to repeat itself within us. When we wake in the morning our heart is saying the *dhikr*, while we are talking to someone His name is repeating itself within us. It is said, "first you do the *dhikr* and then the *dhikr* does you." It becomes a part of our unconscious and sings in our bloodstream. This is beautifully illustrated in an old Sufi story:

> Sahl said to one of his disciples: "Try to say continuously for one day: '*Allâh! Allâh! Allâh!*' and do the same the next day and the day after, until it becomes a habit." Then he told him to repeat it at night also, until it became so familiar that the disciple repeated it even during his sleep. Then Sahl said, "Do not consciously repeat the Name any more, but let your whole faculties be engrossed in remembering Him!" The disciple did this until he became absorbed in the thought of God. One day, a piece of wood fell on his head and broke it. The drops of blood that dripped to the ground bore the legend, "*Allâh! Allâh! Allâh!*"[9]

The way that the name of God permeates the wayfarer is not metaphoric, but a literal happening. The *dhikr* is magnetized by the teacher so that it inwardly aligns the wayfarer with the path and the goal. It is for this reason that the *dhikr* needs to be given by a teacher, though in some instances it can also be given by the Higher Self or, traditionally, by Khidr.

Working in the unconscious the *dhikr* alters our mental, psychological and physical bodies. On the mental level this is easily apparent. Normally, in our everyday life, the mind follows its automatic thinking process, over which we often have very little control. The mind thinks us, rather than the other way 'round. Just catch your mind for a moment and observe its thoughts. Every thought creates a new thought, and every answer a new question. And because energy follows thought, our mental and psychological energy is scattered in many directions. Spiritual life means learning to become one-pointed, to focus all our energy in one direction, towards Him. Through continually repeating His name we alter the grooves of our mental conditioning, the grooves which like those on a record play the same tune over and over again, repeat the same patterns which bind us in our mental habits. The *dhikr* gradually replaces these old grooves with the single groove of His name. The automatic thinking process is redirected towards Him. Like a computer we are reprogrammed for God.

It is said that what you think, you become. If we continually think of Allâh we become one with Allâh. But the effect of the *dhikr* is both more subtle and more powerful than solely an act of mental focusing. One of the secrets of a *dhikr* (or mantra) is that it is a sacred word which conveys the essence of that which it names. This is "the mystery of the identity of God and His Name"[10] ("In the beginning was the Word, and the Word was with God and the Word was God"). In our common everyday language there is not this identity. The word "chair" does not contain the essence of a chair. It merely signifies a chair. But the sacred language of a *dhikr* is different; the vibrations of the word resonate with that which it names, linking the two together. Thus it is able to directly connect the individual with that which it names.

He, the Great Beloved, cannot be named, because any name is a limitation. He is without form and without name, just as it is written of the Tao:

> The Tao that can be told is not the eternal Tao.
> The name that can be named is not the eternal
> name.[11]

And yet mankind calls upon Him in many different ways, and in whatever way He is called, He will answer. Thus the Sufi says, "In the name of Him who has no name, but who appears by whatever name you call Him." If you call Him by the name of Christ, He will appear as Christ, if you call upon Him as Ram, He will appear as Ram. But the name of Allâh is loved by the Sufis because it is closest to the nothingness which is His essence. This name is an opening onto His divine essence, allowing His servants to come closer to Him. It can evoke His presence within the heart, helping us to remember Him and in remembering Him become united with Him, become lost in His nothingness.

PSYCHOLOGICAL AND PHYSICAL TRANSFORMATION

On a psychological level the *dhikr* is a powerful agent of transformation. Working in the unconscious it both realigns our psychic structure and transforms its energies. The *dhikr* is an archetypal sound and word symbol which is magnetically aligned with the path. Archetypal symbols have a specific psychological function: they act as transformers of psychic energy. They convert the *libido* (the instinctual life force) from a "lower" into a "higher" form. As an archetypal symbol, the *dhikr* has the potential to arouse, concentrate and transmute the energies of the unconscious. It disentangles and frees us from the knots and psychological blocks with which we have consciously and unconsciously enchained ourselves, due to our desires, prejudices and the accumulated effects of our attachments and conditioning. One of the most visible examples of this transformative process is the effect that the *dhikr* can have on fear or anxiety, feelings which so often attack the wayfarer. The repetition of His name can so often help in dissolving these feelings or loosening the hold they have on us.

I have found the *dhikr* particularly helpful in dealing with difficult psychological problems. When a painful problem or psychological block comes to the surface, rather than attempting to solve it, I try to stay within the pain or problem and through saying His name offer it to Him. I have found that this effects a process of transformation that is much more dynamic than normal psychological work. It is also very helpful to be able to focus on the Beloved through saying the *dhikr* when immersed in the darkness, chaos and pain of the unconscious. Repeating His name is a powerful light with which one can confront the darkness of the shadow without fear of being overwhelmed or lost. Furthermore, the *dhikr* itself transforms the darkness at the highest level, and it lessens any ego-identification with the work. Embracing an inner difficulty with His name you experience that the work of transformation is done by Another.

The process of transformation also embraces the physical body of the wayfarer. Every atom of creation unknowingly sings His name and longs to be reunited with Him. The *dhikr* infuses this unconscious remembrance with the light of consciousness, with the conscious desire of the lover to remember his Beloved. The light hidden in the darkness of matter responds to the call of this continual prayer and begins to reverberate at a higher frequency. Thus the physical body becomes gradually aligned with the higher consciousness of the Self; the atoms begin to resonate with the song of a soul going home. This transformation was beautifully imaged in a dream in which the dreamer's body first became a heart and then the cells became musical notes:

> I dreamed that my body transformed into a human heart with all of its chambers. The heart travelled in a vast universe. As the heart travelled it would turn inside out and outside in, not missing a beat in between. The voyage was endless with the heart tumbling through space like a large asteroid.
>
> Then the cells of my body began taking the form of blue and gold musical notes. At first the cells were each slowly changing into the blue and gold notes. The rate and number of cells transforming into notes then progressed rapidly until my whole body was composed of the blue and gold notes.
>
> It was as if I were above my body watching this transformation. As this process progressed my body became less and less distinct and more and more formless. There was a blue and gold glow as my body and the musical notes became less distinct.
>
> I awakened, and had an extremely calm feeling. As I awakened, the borders of my body felt beyond their usual boundaries, gradually returning to their usual boundaries.

Within our heart we are united with the Beloved. Our heartbeat is part of the great rhythm of creation. But for most people this is like a memory buried so deep we have forgotten it. When we consciously aspire to remember Him the practice of meditation and the *dhikr* awaken this pre-existing state of oneness. Our heart opens and we begin to feel how its rhythm is attuned to the song of the universe. Slowly this inner attunement resonates throughout the whole body, and every cell becomes a note in the symphony of creation. From the depths of the heart to the fingertips and the soles of the feet every part of us unites in the one song which is creation's offering to the Creator.

The *dhikr* transforms the wayfarer and takes him home. One of its secrets is that if it has become automatic, then, at the moment of death, with your very last breath you will call out His name. It is said that the last thought of a dying person determines where that person goes. Inayat Khan gives as an example the person whose last thought is her grandmother's jewelry, and who therefore comes back to this world to experience this jewelry. But if your final thought is Allâh, His name will take you to Him.

THE PRIMORDIAL COVENANT

The *dhikr* is a continual prayer of remembrance that reconnects the lover with the Beloved. At its deepest level it is an activation of the primordial covenant when the Beloved asked, "Am I not your Lord?" and humanity responded, "Yes, we witness it." This response was the first *dhikr*, secreted in the hearts of his lovers. The saying of the *dhikr* in time and space, with each and every breath, reminds the lover of his eternal pledge to witness the Beloved. The *dhikr* activates this secret covenant imprinted within the heart which contains the essence of the lover's relationship with the Beloved—the experience of our primordial state of union.

This covenant is an archetypal experience buried deep within the unconscious. When the *dhikr* activates this covenant, our primal consciousness of the Beloved begins to infuse its light into the depths and gradually permeate the unconscious. Our conscious aspiration to remember Him is like a catalyst that activates a dormant archetype: the light of our aspiration evokes the light hidden in the depths. It is the archetypal *dhikr*, the covenant of the soul, that is the most powerful agent of transformation, for it speaks to us of our own experience, our own deepest bond with the Beloved.

We say the *dhikr* because we are separate from Him and long to return to Him; the *dhikr* reminds us of "what we were before we were." This state of remembrance is the consciousness of the soul. In saying the *dhikr* we bring this atemporal consciousness into the dimension of time and space. Thus our everyday life becomes charged with the vibration of this higher consciousness; it begins to sing the song of the soul. As the *dhikr* resonates in the unconscious and permeates every cell of our body, so the link of love that joins the Creator to the creation resonates with the song of remembrance. The lover brings this quality of consciousness into his life and into the world.

The *dhikr* gradually dissolves the illusion of separation, and the loneliness of the path is replaced by the feeling of His companionship, for God has promised, "I am the companion of him who recollects Me."[12] In a culture which suffers so deeply from the feeling of separation and His absence, the experience of His companionship is of tremendous importance not only to the lover. Spiritual experiences are never given just for ourselves; they are for others. His presence carries a scent that reminds others of what the world has forgotten. It seeks out the hearts of those who are lonely for Him, and tells them that what they long for is possible.

At the primordial covenant spiritual nourishment was given to humanity, what the Persian poets call the "banquet of *alast*."[13] This nourishment is hidden within the heart and is only accessible when we remember our pledge and witness Him. It is the food that the pilgrim longs for; it can be found in the company of lovers, in groups of sincere seekers. For when a group collectively remembers the Beloved then that nourishment is present. Irina Tweedie has said that coming to the group was like "charging the batteries," getting the spiritual energy to sustain us in the world. This energy is the mana that feeds us as we walk along our lonely road.

When we practice remembrance we begin to recognize the Creator reflected in the creation. Then consciousness is infused with the energy of the Self and the deepest purpose of creation becomes known within the heart. At the present time humanity's soul is starving because we have forgotten our sense of purpose, and the shadow of material progress stands in our way. Trying to feed the soul with the promise of technology only emphasizes the pain of separation from the source. Through their work of remembrance His lovers can help to align our collective consciousness with the source of life and the real nourishment we need.

RECONNECTING THE MANY WITH THE ONE

For so long we have collectively identified ourselves with our actions, with what we do rather than what we are. We value ourselves by the external result of our actions, by what we create in the outer world. Yet true purpose and meaning come from deep within the unconscious, from the archetypal world that is the guardian of these values. The meaning of Hestia, goddess of the hearth, does not come from the outer actions of cooking, cleaning and caring for the house. The lack of fulfillment that many women feel in these "chores" points to Hestia's absence. These activities are only meaningful when there is a relationship to the goddess that honors the home. We need to remember what as a culture we have forgotten: it is the inner connection that gives value and purpose to our life.

There are many gods and goddesses, many different archetypes underlying the diverse aspects of our lives. Each has its purpose and meaning; each its light and dark side—Aphrodite, goddess of love, as well as Athena, goddess of war. But underlying this diversity is a tremendous unity, because, "There is no god but God." This unity does not deny the multiplicity, but embraces it, just as the name Allâh includes all His divine and beautiful attributes.

At the beginning it may be necessary to turn away from the many in order to focus on the One, but later it is necessary to experience the One within the many. In the past age polytheism was banished by monotheism, often with the sword. The temples of the gods and goddesses were destroyed and the mosque and church took their place. But now these ancient energies that were worshipped in the temples have been rediscovered in the unconscious and we can no longer afford to deny them. They are the very foundation of our psychic structure and our relationship to life itself.

The central archetype is the Self, the divine center within the human being that was never separated from the Beloved. The archetype of the Self, "that boundless

Power, source of every power, manifesting itself as life,"[14] contains within it all the other archetypes, just as the name Allâh contains all of His divine names. Through the *dhikr* we affirm our own relationship to the Beloved who is within our own heart. Within the heart we make a conscious connection with the Self, and thus with the whole pantheon of gods and goddesses. Through re-membering Him we align ourselves with our own essence and thus with every archetype. We return to the deepest source from which all life flows. And because we are not separate from life, we do this work not just for ourselves, but for life itself. We begin to reconnect the many with the One.

As the *dhikr* is activated in the unconscious the most ancient memory of the primordial covenant stirs within us. We begin to reconnect with humanity's primal purpose, the act of witnessing. This is the deepest meaning of life, and the real purpose of consciousness. When we witness Him we include in that moment every aspect of creation, every leaf, every flower and every fish. When His name sings in our heart we embrace the whole world and feel its unity. This is one of the secrets of the *dhikr*: we experience His oneness because everything is imprinted with His name. In these moments we give to the world the conscious knowledge of its own unity and help to heal the world's sense of alienation.

COMPANIONSHIP

For the lover there is a deep joy in repeating the name of his invisible Beloved who is so near and yet so far. When He is near it is wonderful to be able to thank Him for the bliss of His presence, for the sweetness of His companionship. When He is absent it helps us to bear the longing and the pain, for we can cry out to Him with every breath. In times of trouble His name brings reassurance and help. It gives us strength and can help to dissolve the blocks that separate us from Him. When we say His name He is with us, even if we feel so alone with our burdens. He helps His servant whenever He can, and in times of great need His name can save us.

A friend who had learnt to say His name had a very difficult relationship with a man she loved. He had been caught in the self-destructive grip of drugs and would often be in a state of paranoia. One day, while under the influence of drugs, he took her for a drive in the country and began to blame her for all his troubles. Stopping the car beside a field he took a gun he kept with him and forced her out of the car. He held the gun to her head, intending to shoot her. She knew that this was no empty threat and all she could do was cry, "Allâh." The moment she cried His name a change came over the man. His paranoia disappeared and he gave her the gun, asking her to keep it away from him. He was deeply sorry for his actions, and asked her to drive him back home.

Allâh loves those who love Him. He remembers those who remember Him. Through the *dhikr* we bring into consciousness the bond we always had with Him and become aware of the deeper secrets of our real unity. The name which we repeat is the name by which we knew Him before we were born. It is the name engraven into our hearts. The *dhikr* brings the imprint of the heart into the world of time and also leads us back to Him. Gradually we become conscious of the depth of our connection and how in our hearts we are always united.

The name reveals that which it names, and the lover begins to see that there is nothing other than God:

> God made this name [Allâh] a mirror for man,
> so that when he looks in it, he knows the true
> meaning of "God was and there was naught
> beside Him," and in that moment it is revealed to
> him that his hearing is God's hearing, his sight is
> God's sight, his speech is God's speech, his life is
> God's life, his knowledge is God's knowledge, his
> will God's will and his power God's power. . .[15]

Through repeating His name the lover becomes identified with his Beloved who had been hidden within his own heart. The Beloved loves to hear His name on the lips and in the hearts of His servants, and in response gradually removes the veils that keep Him hidden. Then the lover finds Him not only secreted within the heart, but also in the outer world, for "whithersoever ye turn, there is the Face of God."[16]

The Beloved becomes the constant companion of the lover. The lover also becomes the companion of God, for the "eyes which regard God are also the eyes through which He regards the world."[17] This relationship of companionship belongs to the beyond and yet it is lived in this world. It is the deepest friendship and it demands the total participation of the lover. We are His servants, and He loves to be known as "the servant of His servants."

Through the *dhikr* we attune our whole being to the frequency of love. We embrace the pain of separation as well as the joy of knowing Him from whom we are separated. We say the name of our Beloved because it reminds us of Him for whom we long. When Allâh cries from the heart it is both our prayer and the answer to our prayer. We cry to Him because we have not forgotten Him. To always remember Him here, in this world, is to always be with Him. The heart knows this, even if the mind and ego do not. Rûmî tells the story of a devotee who was praying when Satan appeared to him and said:

> "How long wilt thou cry 'O Allâh?' Be quiet for thou wilt get no answer."
>
> The devotee hung his head in silence. After a while he had a vision of the prophet Khidr, who said to him, "Ah, why hast thou ceased to call on God?"
>
> "Because the answer, 'Here I am' came not," he replied.
>
> Khidr said, "God hath ordered me to go to thee and say this:
>
> 'Was it not I that summoned thee to my service?
> Did I not make thee busy with my name?
> Thy calling "Allâh!" was my "Here I am,"
> Thy yearning pain My messenger to thee.
> Of all those tears and cries and supplications
> I was the magnet, and I gave them wings.'"[18]

The same story was told in a woman's dream in which she was howling at the moon and felt a terrible failure and despair because there was no answer. Later she realized the deepest intimacy of love, which is that our cry is His cry to Himself. In crying out to Him we share in the mystery of His creation, which is that He who was One and Alone wanted to be loved, and so He created the world.

Our longing and our cry to Him are the stamp of our companionship with Him. We are His lovers and we look to Him. As we turn our hearts and look towards Him we do the "one thing needful." We bring into consciousness the pledge we made at the primordial covenant. We recognize both for ourselves and for the whole world the link of love that unites the Creator with his creation. And we abandon ourselves to love:

Verily there are servants among my servants who love Me, and I love them, and they long for Me, and I long for them and they look at Me, and I look at them . . . . And their signs are that they preserve the shade at daytime as compassionately as a herdsman preserves his sheep, and they long for sunset as the bird longs for his nest at dusk, and when the night comes and the shadows become mixed and the beds are spread out and the bedsteads are put up and every lover is alone with his beloved, then they will stand on their feet and put their faces on the ground and will call Me with My word and will flatter Me with My graces, half crying and half weeping, half bewildered and half complaining, sometimes standing, sometimes sitting, sometimes kneeling, sometimes prostrating, and I see what they bear for My sake and I hear what they complain from My love.[19]

Meditation

In this meditation we have to imagine three things:

    1. We must suppose that we go deep within ourselves, deeper and deeper into our most hidden self. There in our innermost being, in the very core of ourselves, we will find a place where there is peace, stillness and, above all, love.

    God is Love, says the Sufi. Human beings are all love, for they are made in His image; only they have forgotten it long ago. When we love another human being, however deeply, there is a place in our heart where this beloved human has no access. There, we are quite alone. But within us there is a longing, which is the ultimate proof that this place is reserved for Him alone.

    2. After having found this place, we must imagine that we are seated there, immersed into, surrounded by, the Love of God. We are in deepest peace. We are loved; we are sheltered; we are secure. All of us is there, physical body and all; nothing is outside, not even a fingertip, not even the tiniest hair. Our whole being is contained within the Love of God.

3. As we sit there, happy, serene in His Presence, thoughts will intrude into our mind—what we did the day before, what we have to do tomorrow. Memories float by, images appear before the mind's eye.

We have to imagine that we are getting hold of every thought, every image and feeling, and drowning it, merging it into the feeling of love.

Every feeling, especially the feeling of love, is much more dynamic than the thinking process, so if one does this practice well, with the utmost concentration, all thoughts will disappear. Nothing will remain. The mind will be empty.[1]

Notes

INTRODUCTION, pages xi–xvi

1. Quoted by Evelyn Underhill, *Mysticism*, p. 356.
2. "De Septem Gradibus Amoris," chap. xiv, quoted by Underhill, p. 435.
3. The Blessed John Ruysbroeck, quoted by Underhill, p. 435.
4. Quoted by Miriam and José Argüelles, *The Feminine*, p. 123.
5. Quoted by Annemarie Schimmel, *Mystical Dimensions of Islam*, p. 139.
6. Henry Corbin, *The Man of Light in Iranian Sufism*, p. 57.
7. *St. Luke*, 10:42.
8. Underhill, p. 130.

THE SHADOW SIDE OF SPIRITUAL LIFE, pages 1–27

1. Dhu'l-Nûn was asked: "What is the end of the mystic?" He answered: "When he is as he was where he was before he was." Quoted by A.J. Arberry, *The Doctrine of the Sufis*, p. 152.
2. Ghalib, trans. Jane Hirshfield, *The Enlightened Heart*, ed. Stephen Mitchell, p. 106.
3. Annemarie Schimmel, *Mystical Dimensions of Islam*, p. 24.
4. *The Odes of Ibnu 'l-Fârid*, trans. R.A. Nicholson, *Studies in Islamic Mysticism*, p. 184.
5. Rûmî, quoted by Connie Zweig and Jeremiah Abrams, *Meeting the Shadow*, p. 80.
6. Quoted by R.A. Nicholson, *The Mystics of Islam*, p. 31.
7. Jeanne Guyon, *Spiritual Torrents*, p. 1.
8. Rûmî, *Mathnawî*, 1:132.
9. Rûmî, trans. Andrew Harvey, *Love's Fire*, p. 77.
10. Quoted by Schimmel, *Mystical Dimensions of Islam*, p.72.

11. *Discourses of Rûmî*, trans. A.J. Arberrry, quoted by William C. Chittick, *The Sufi Path of Love*, p. 54.

12. Irina Tweedie, *Daughter of Fire*, p. 227

13. *De Vera religione*, XXXIX, 72.

14. Quoted by Nicholson, *Studies in Islamic Mysticism*, p. 56.

15. Râbi'a, trans. Charles Upton, *The Doorkeeper of the Heart*, p. 52.

16. Quoted by Zweig and Abrams, p. 128.

17. Quoted by Schimmel, *Mystical Dimensions of Islam,* p. 133.

18. See Vaughan-Lee, *The Call and the Echo*, pp. 132-138.

19. Quoted by Schimmel, *Mystical Dimensions of Islam*, p. 283.

20. C.G. Jung, *Collected Works 9ii (Aion)*, para. 142.

PREGNANT WITH GOD, pages 28 - 56

1. Tweedie, p. 793.

2. Rûmî, quoted by Chittick, p. 303.

3. Tweedie, unpublished quotation.

4. Eva de Vitray-Meyerovitch, *Rûmî and Sufism*, p. 128, author's italics.

5. T.S. Eliot, "Burnt Norton," ll. 42-3.

6. *St. Matthew*, 22.14.

7. Tweedie, p. 671.

8. Chittick, p. 162.

9. Rûmî, "A Thief in the Night," trans. Peter Lamborn Wilson and Nasrollah Pourjavady, *The Drunken Universe*, p. 104.

10. See Introduction, note 6.

11. Kabir, adapted from *Songs of Kabir*, p. 56.

12. Tweedie, p. 169.

13. Vitray-Meyerovitch, p. 128.

14. T.S. Eliot, "East Coker," ll. 112-121.

15. Ruysbroeck, *The Adornment of the Spiritual Marriage*, quoted by F.C. Happold, *Mysticism*, p. 293.

16. Schimmel, *Mystical Dimensions of Islam*, p. 146.

17. Quoted by Matthew Fox, *The Coming of the Cosmic Christ*, p. 118.

18. *The Enlightened Heart*, ed. Stephen Mitchell, p. 87.
19. See Meditation, pp. 134-5.
20. *Katha Upanishad*, trans. W.B. Yeats, Book 2, 1.
21. Angelius Silesius, *The Enlightened Heart*, p. 89.
22. Rûmî, quoted by Chittick, p. 389.
23. *Adornment of the Spiritual Marriage*, quoted by Underhill, p. 345 and pp. 333-4.
24. Quoted by Fox, p. 36.
25. Unpublished quotation.
26. See pp. 22-3 and p. 23 note 18.

STAGES OF PRAYER Part One:
THE BIRTH OF THE BELOVED, pages 57–79

1. Gerard Manley Hopkins, "I wake and feel the fell of dark not day." ll. 6-8, *The Poems and Prose of Gerard Manley Hopkins*.
2. Tweedie, p. 404.
3. Farîd ud-Dîn Attâr, *The Conference of the Birds*, trans. C.S. Nott, p. 33.
4. "On the First Degree of Prayer," quoted by F. C. Happold, *Mysticism,* p. 345.
5. Tweedie, unpublished quotation.
6. Tweedie, p. 79.
7. Hopkins, "No worst, there is none. Pitched past pitch of grief," ll. 3-4.
8. Sanâ'i, quoted by Javad Nurbakhsh, *Sufi Symbolism*, Volume 2, p. 121.
9. Quoted by Schimmel, *Mystical Dimensions of Islam*, p. 72.
10. Quoted by Happold, pp. 346-7.
11. Quoted by Happold, p. 346.
12. Quoted in *Four Sufi Classics*, p. 191.
13. *Anatomy of the Psyche*, p. 6.
14. Quoted by Nurbakhsh, *Sufi Symbolism*, Volume 1, p. 80.
15. Quoted by Annemarie Schimmel, *I Am Wind, You Are Fire*, p. 88.
16. Abû Sa'îd ibn Abî'l-Khayr.
17. Quoted by Schimmel, *Mystical Dimensions of Islam*, p. 135.

18. Quoted by Schimmel, *Mystical Dimensions of Islam*, p. 69.

19. Tweedie, p. 519.

20. Tweedie, unpublished lecture, Schwarzsee, Switzerland, 1988.

21. Tweedie, unpublished lecture, Schwarzsee, Switzerland, 1988.

22. Rûmî, quoted by Chittick, p. 339.

23. Tweedie, p. 200.

24. Robert Johnson, *Femininity Lost and Regained*, p. 27.

25. Johnson, p. 27.

26. Nurbakhsh, *Sufi Symbolism*, Volume 2, p. 114.

27. *Song of Solomon*, 5:5-6.

28. Quoted by Corbin, pp. 21-22.

29. Jeanne Guyon, *The Song of the Bride*, p. 110.

30. Al-Hallâj, quoted by Schimmel, *Mystical Dimensions of Islam*, p. 165.

31. Quoted by Schimmel, *I Am Wind, You Are Fire*, p. 172.

32. Quoted by James Arraj, *St. John of the Cross and Dr. C.G. Jung*, p. 60.

33. Sermon, "Blessed are the Poor."

34. Muhâsibî, quoted by R. S. Bhatnagar, *Dimensions of Classical Sufi Thought*, p. 49.

STAGES OF PRAYER Part Two:
LIVING IN THE TWO WORLDS, pages 80–101

1. *The Bhagavad Gita*, trans. Juan Mascaro, 4:24.

2. Quoted by Underhill, p. 436

3. Quoted by Happold, p. 351.

4. Sukie Colgrave, *By Way of Pain*, p.44.

5. *C.G. Jung, Emma Jung, and Toni Wolff, A Collection of Remembrances*, ed. Ferne Jensen, p. 52.

6. *St. Matthew*, 7:6

7. *King Lear*, V ii 9.

8. *Katha Upanishad*, Book 2, 1.

9. Sura 41:53, quoted by Schimmel, *Mystical Dimensions of Islam*, p. 188.

10. Joseph Campell, *The Power of Myth*, p. 120.

11. Colgrave, p. 89.

12. Tweedie, p. 338.

13. e.e. cummings, 38 "silently if, out of not knowable," *73 poems.*

14. Qur'an, Sura 18: 64-81. Also Llewellyn Vaughan-Lee, *The Call and the Echo*, pp. 6-8.

15. Corbin, p. 100.

16. Quoted in *Home Planet*, ed. Kevin Kelley.

17. Quoted in Roger Housden, *The Fire in the Heart*, p. 162.

18. Quoted on the record sleeve of *Gothic Verses, Sequences and Hymns by Abbess Hildegard of Bingen*, Hyperion.

19. *Interior Castle*, p. 106.

20. Yahyâ ebn Ma'âdh, quoted by Javad Nurbakhsh, *Spiritual Poverty in Sufism*, p. 15.

21. See Corbin, p. 76.

22. *Hadîth qudsî*, quoted by Schimmel, *Mystical Dimensions of Islam*, p. 133.

23. See Vaughan-Lee, p. 146.

24. Saint Theresa, *Interior Castle*, p. 109.

25. Quoted by Nurbakhsh, *Spiritual Poverty in Sufism*, p. 13.

26. "Mother Teresa sees herself as God's pencil," Tribune News Services, date unknown.

27. Tweedie, p. 349.

28. Quoted by Housden, p. 167.

29. e.e. cummings, "i carry your heart with me(i carry it in," *Selected Poems 1923-1958.*

30. Ibn 'Arabî, quoted by Corbin, p. 22.

31. "The Dry Salvages," l. 93.

STAGES OF PRAYER Part Three:
ECSTASY, pages 102–115

1. Hopkins, "God's Grandeur".

2. Sura 24:41

3. *Collected Works 7*, para. 519.

4. Quoted by Schimmel, *Mystical Dimensions of Islam*, p. 266.

5. *Katha Upanishad*, Book 2, 1.
6. Quoted by Underhill, p. 233.
7. Quoted by Underhill, p. 64.
8. Tweedie, unpublished lecture, "The Paradox of Mysticism," Wrekin Trust "Mystics and Scientists Conference," 1985.
9. Farîd ud-Dîn 'Attâr, *The Conference of the Birds*, trans. C.S. Nott, p. 122.
10. Quoted by Underhill, p. 372.
11. Quoted by Happold, p. 354.
12. Quoted by Happold, p. 352.
13. *The Cloud of Unknowing*, Chapter 8, quoted by Happold, p. 312.

THE DHIKR, pages 116–133

1. Tweedie, p. 730.
2. Hamid Algar, "A Brief History of the Naqshbandi Order," *The Naqshbandis*, ed. by Marc Gaborieau, Alexandre Popovic and Thierry Zarcome, p. 9.
3. Johan G.J. ter Haar, "The Importance of the Spiritual Guide in the Naqshbandi Order," *The Legacy of Mediaeval Persian Sufism*, ed. by Leonard Lewisohn, p. 316.
4. The equilvalent of the *dhikr* in the Christian tradition is the Jesus prayer, "Lord Jesus Christ, have Mercy on Me." Like the *dhikr* it is said with the breath. See *The Way of a Pilgrim*, esp. pp. 60-66.
5. Qur'an, 6:91. Quoted by Nicholson, *Studies in Islamic Mysticism*, p. 10.
6. Nicholson, *Studies in Islamic Mysticism*, p. 7.
7. Tweedie, p. 775.
8. Trans. Daniel Liebert, *Rumi, Fragments, Ecstasies*, p. 45.
9. Schimmel, *Mystical Dimensions of Islam*, p. 169.
10. Peter Lamborn Wilson and Nasrollah Pourjavady, *The Drunken Universe*, p. 45.
11. Lao Tsu, *Tao Te Ching*, trans. Gia-Fu Feng and Jane English, 1.
12. *Hadîth qudsî*, quoted by Schimmel, *Mystical Dimensions of Islam*, p. 168.

13. Schimmel, *Mystical Dimensions of Islam*, p. 172.
14. *Katha Upanishad*, Book 2, 1.
15. Nicholson, *Studies in Islamic Mysticism*, p. 93.
16. Qur'an 2:109, quoted by Ibn 'Arabî, *"Whoso Knoweth Himself..."* (from the *Treatise on Being*), p. 9.
17. Schimmel, *Mystical Dimensions of Islam*, p. 203.
18. Quoted by Nicholson, *The Mystics of Islam*, p. 113.
19. Al-Ghâzzalî, quoted by Schimmel, *Mystical Dimensions of Islam*, p. 139.

MEDITATION, pages 134–135

1. Tweedie, pp. 821-2.

Selected Bibliography

'Arabî, Ibn. *"Whoso Knoweth Himself..."*. Abingdon, Oxon: Beshara Publications, 1976.

Arberry, A.J. *The Doctrine of the Sufis*. Lahore: Sh. Muhammad Ashraf, 1966.

Argüelles, Miriam & José. *The Feminine*. Boulder: Shambala Publications, 1977.

Arraj, James. *St. John of the Cross and Dr. C. G. Jung*. Chiloquin, Oregon: Inner Growth Books, 1986.

Attâr, Farîd ud-Dîn. *The Conference of the Birds*. Trans. C.S. Nott. London: Routledge & Kegan Paul, 1961.

The Bhagavad Gita. Trans. Juan Mascaro. Harmondsworth: Penquin Books, 1962.

Bhatnagar, R.S. *Dimensions of Classical Sufi Thought*. Delhi: Motilal Banarsidass, 1984.

The Bible, Authorized Version. London: 1611.

Campell, Joseph. *The Power of Myth*. London: Doubleday, 1989.

Chittick, William C. *The Sufi Path of Love*. Albany: State University of New York Press, 1983.

Colgrave, Sukie. *By Way of Pain: A Passage into Self*. Rochester, Vermont: Park Street Press, 1988.

Corbin, Henry. *The Man of Light in Iranian Sufism*. London: Shambala Publications, 1978.

cummings, e.e. *Selected Poems 1923-1958*. London: Faber and Faber, 1960.

——. *73 Poems*. London: Faber and Faber, 1964.

Edinger, Edward. *The Anatomy of the Psyche*. La Salle: Open Court, 1985.

Eliot, T.S. *Collected Poems*. London: Faber and Faber, 1963.

Fox, Matthew. *The Coming of the Cosmic Christ*. San Francisco: Harper & Row, 1988.

Gaborieau, Marc; Popovic, Alexandre et Zarcone, Thierry, ed. *Naqshbandis*. Istanbul: l'Institut Francçais d'Etudes Anatoliennes d'Istanbul, 1990.

Guyon, Jeanne. *Spiritual Torrents*. Auburn, Maine: The Seed Sowers, 1990.

143

————. *The Song of the Bride*. Auburn, Maine: The Seed Sowers, 1990.

Harvey, Andrew. *Love's Fire, Re-Creations of Rumi*. Ithaca, New York: Meerama, 1989.

Hopkins, Gerard Manley. *The Poems and Prose of Gerard Manley Hopkins*. Harmondsworth: Penguin Books, 1953.

Housden, Roger. *Fire In the Heart*. Shaftesbury: Element Books, 1990.

Jensen, Ferne, ed. *C.G. Jung, Emma Jung, and Toni Wolff: A Collection of Remembrances*. San Francisco: The Analytical Club of San Francisco, 1982.

Johnson, Robert. *Femininity Lost and Regained*. New York: Harper & Row, 1990.

Jung, C.G. *Collected Works*. London: Routledge & Kegan Paul.

Kabir. *Songs of Kabir*. Trans. Rabindranath Tagore. New York: Samuel Weiser, 1977.

Kelley, Kevin, ed. *The Home Planet*. Reading, Massachusetts: Addison-Wesley Publishing Company, 1988.

The Koran. Trans. N.J. Dawood. London: Penguin Books, 1956.

Lao Tsu. *Tao Te Ching*. Trans. Gia-Fu Feng and Jane English. Aldershot: Wildwood House Ltd., 1973.

Lewisohn, Lewis, ed. *The Legacy of Mediaeval Persian Sufism*. London: Khaniqahi Nimatullahi Publications, 1992.

Liebert, Daniel. *Rumi: Fragments, Ecstasies*. Santa Fe, New Mexico: Source Books, 1981.

Mitchell, Stephen, ed. *The Enlightened Heart*. New York: Harper & Row, 1989.

Nicholson, R.A. *Studies in Islamic Mysticism*. Cambridge: Cambridge University Press, 1921.

————. *The Mystics of Islam*. London: Arkana, 1989.

Nurbakhsh, Javad. *Sufi Symbolism* Volumes I - IV. London: Khaniqahi-Nimatullahi Publications, 1984-1990.

————. *Spiritual Poverty in Sufism*. London: Khaniqahi-Nimatullahi Publications, 1984.

Pendlebury, David, trans. *Four Sufi Classics*. London: Octagon Press, 1982.

Savin, Olga, trans. *The Way of a Pilgrim*. Boston: Shambala Publications, 1991.

Schimmel, Annemarie. *Mystical Dimensions of Islam.* Chapel Hill: University of North Carolina Press, 1975.

——. *I Am Wind, You Are Fire.* Boston: Shambala Publications, 1992.

Shakespeare, William. *King Lear.* Ed. Kenneth Muir. London: Methuen & Company, 1952.

Teresa of Avila. *Interior Castle.* New York: Doubleday, 1989.

Tweedie, Irina. *Daughter of Fire, A Diary of a Spiritual Training with a Sufi Master.* Nevada City: Blue Dolphin Publishing, 1986.

Underhill, Evelyn. *Mysticism.* New York: New American Library, 1974.

Upton, Charles. *Doorkeeper of the Heart, Versions of Râbi'a.* Putney, Vermont: Threshold Books, 1988.

Vaughan-Lee, Llewellyn. *The Lover and the Serpent: Dreamwork within a Sufi Tradition.* Shaftesbury: Element Books, 1989.

——. *The Call and the Echo: Sufi Dreamwork and the Psychology of the Beloved.* Putney, Vermont: Threshold Books, 1992.

Vitray-Meyerovitch, Eva de. *Rûmî and Sufism.* Sausalito, California: The Post-Apollo Press, 1987.

Wilson, Peter Lamborn and Pourjavady, Nasrollah. *The Drunken Universe.* Grand Rapids: Phanes Press, 1987.

Zweig, Connie and Abrams, Jeremiah, ed. *Meeting the Shadow.* Los Angeles: Jeremy P. Tarcher, 1990.

Yeats, W.B., trans. (with Shree Purohit Swami). *The Ten Principal Upanishads.* London: Faber and Faber, 1937.

Index

Acknowledgments

For permission to use copyrighted material, the author gratefully wishes to acknowledge: Gower Publishing Company, for permission to quote from *Tao Te Ching* translated by Gia-Fu Feng and Jane English; Harper-Collins Publishers, for permission to quote from *The Enlightened Heart* edited by Stephen Mitchell, copyright © 1989 by Stephen Mitchell; Khaniqahi Nimatullahi Publications, for permission to quote from *Sufi Symbolism, Volume One & Volume Two*, by Dr. Javad Nurbakhsh; Daniel Liebert, for permission to quote from *Rumi, Fragments, Ecstasies*, translated by Daniel Liebert; Liveright Publishing Corporation, 500 Fifth Avenue, New York 10110, for permission to quote *'i carry your heart with me(i carry it in"* and the lines from *"silently if,out of not knowable"* are reprinted from *Complete Poems, 1904-1962*, by E.E.Cummings, edited by George J. Firmage, by permission of Liveright Publishing Corporation. Copyright © 1923, 1925-26, 1931, 1935, 1938-40 1944-62 by E.E.Cummings. Copyright © 1961, 1963, 1966-68 by Marion Morehouse Cummings. Copyright © 1972-91 by the Trustees for the E. E. Cummings Trust; Meeramma Publications, 26 Spruce Lane, Ithaca, New York 14850, for permission to quote from *Love's Fire, Re-Creations of Rumi* by Andrew Harvey; Threshold Books, RD 4 Box 600, Putney, Vermont 05346, for permission to quote from *The Doorkeeper of the Heart, Versions of Rabi'a*, translated by Charles Upton.

LLEWELLYN VAUGHAN-LEE, PH.D., is a Sufi teacher in the Naqshbandiyya-Mujaddidiyya Sufi Order. Born in London in 1953, he has followed the Naqshbandi Sufi path since he was nineteen. In 1991 he became the successor of Irina Tweedie, author of *Daughter of Fire: A Diary of a Spiritual Training with a Sufi Master.* He then moved to Northern California and founded The Golden Sufi Center (see www.goldensufi.org). Author of several books, he has specialized in the area of dreamwork, integrating the ancient Sufi approach to dreams with the insights of Jungian Psychology. Since 2000 the focus of his writing and teaching has been on spiritual responsibility in our present time of transition, and an awakening global consciousness of oneness. More recently he has written about the feminine, the *Anima Mundi* (world soul), and spiritual ecology (see www.workingwithoneness.org).

THE GOLDEN SUFI CENTER is a 501(c)(3) California Non-Profit Corporation dedicated to making the teachings of the Naqshbandi Sufi Path available to all seekers. For further information, please contact us at:

THE GOLDEN SUFI CENTER
P.O. Box 456
Point Reyes, California 94956
tel: (415) 663-0100 · *fax:* (415) 663-0103
www.goldensufi.org

LOVE IS A FIRE:
The Sufi's Mystical Journey Home

THE CIRCLE OF LOVE

CATCHING THE THREAD:
Sufism, Dreamwork, and Jungian Psychology

THE FACE BEFORE I WAS BORN:
A Spiritual Autobiography

THE PARADOXES OF LOVE

SUFISM:
The Transformation of the Heart

IN THE COMPANY OF FRIENDS:
Dreamwork within a Sufi Group

THE BOND WITH THE BELOVED:
The Mystical Relationship of the Lover and the Beloved

∽

edited by LLEWELLYN VAUGHAN-LEE
with biographical information by SARA SVIRI

TRAVELLING THE PATH OF LOVE:
Sayings of Sufi Masters

∽

by PETER KINGSLEY

A Story Waiting to Pierce You:
Mongolia, Tibet, and the Destiny of the Western World

Reality

In the Dark Places of Wisdom

⁓

by SARA SVIRI

The Taste of Hidden Things:
Images of the Sufi Path

⁓

by HILARY HART

The Unknown She:
Eight Faces of an Emerging Consciousness

⁓